P9-EML-634

THE UNITED STATES AND CANADA

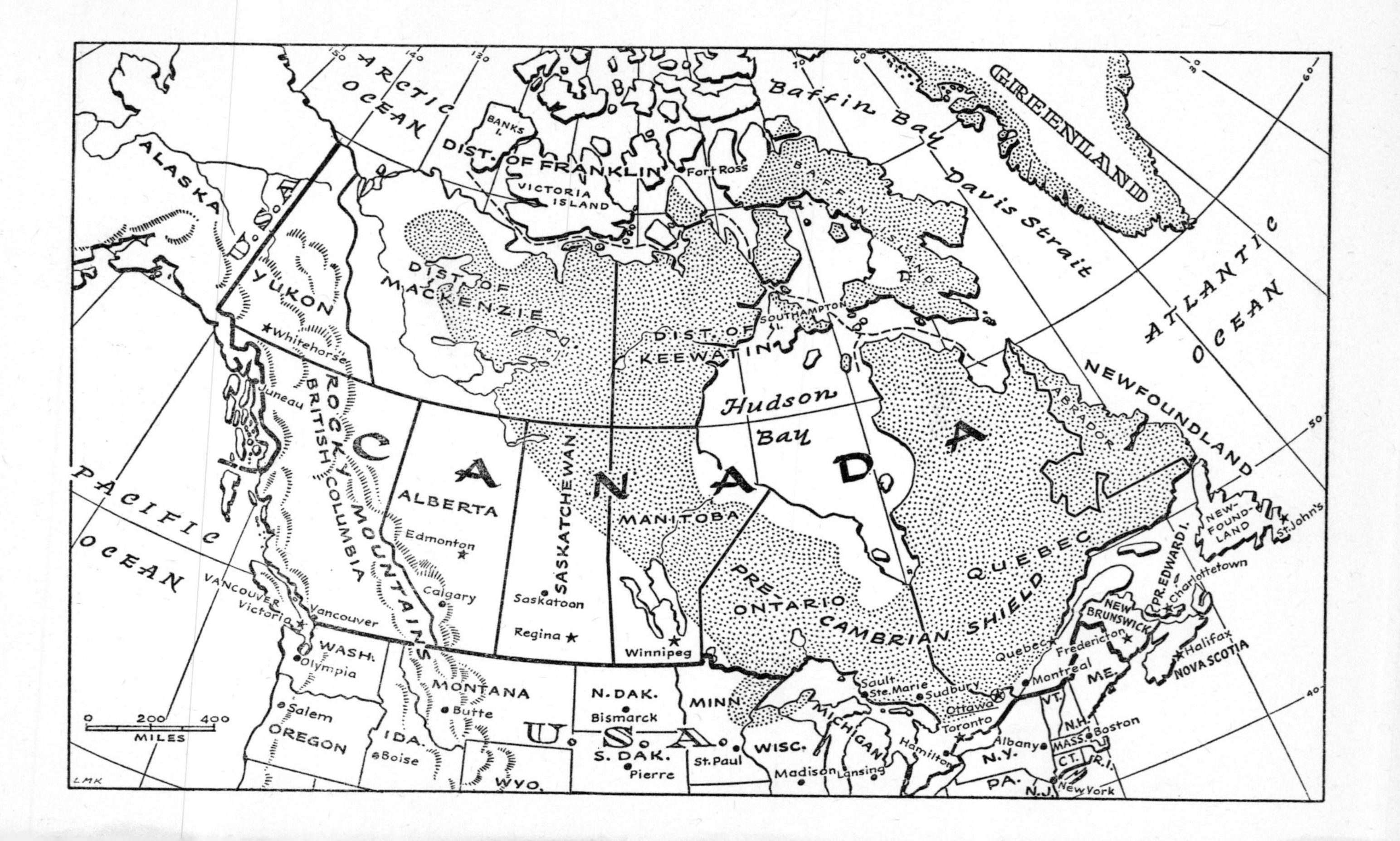
ARCTIC OCEAN
Baffin Bay
Davis Strait
GREENLAND
ATLANTIC OCEAN
PACIFIC OCEAN
ALASKA
U.S.A.
YUKON
Whitehorse
Juneau
DIST. OF FRANKLIN
BANKS I.
VICTORIA ISLAND
Fort Ross
BAFFIN ISLAND
DIST. OF MACKENZIE
DIST. OF KEEWATIN
SOUTHAMPTON I.
Hudson Bay
LABRADOR
NEWFOUNDLAND
NEW-FOUND-LAND
St. John's
CANADA
ROCKY MOUNTAINS
BRITISH COLUMBIA
ALBERTA
Edmonton
Calgary
SASKATCHEWAN
Saskatoon
Regina
MANITOBA
Winnipeg
PRE-CAMBRIAN SHIELD
ONTARIO
QUEBEC
PR. EDWARD I.
Charlottetown
NEW BRUNSWICK
Fredericton
Halifax
NOVA SCOTIA
Quebec
Montreal
Ottawa
Sudbury
Sault Ste. Marie
Toronto
Hamilton
VANCOUVER I.
Vancouver
Victoria
WASH.
Olympia
OREGON
Salem
IDA.
Boise
MONTANA
Butte
WYO.
N. DAK.
Bismarck
S. DAK.
Pierre
MINN
St. Paul
WISC.
Madison
MICHIGAN
Lansing
N.Y.
Albany
PA.
N.J.
New York
VT.
N.H.
MASS.
Boston
CT.
R.I.
ME.
0 200 400
MILES
LMK

The American Assembly, *Columbia University*

THE UNITED STATES AND CANADA

Prentice-Hall, Inc., *Englewood Cliffs, N.J.*

 Library of Congress Catalog Card Number 64-21215. Printed in the United States of America—C. P 93838, C 93839

Preface

Each new American Assembly program opens with a meeting at Arden House, on the Harriman (New York) campus of Columbia University. Seventy-two participants, representative of a variety of occupations and geographical areas, met April 23-26, 1964, for the Twenty-fifth American Assembly on *The United States and Canada.* At the close of their discussions they issued a statement of findings and recommendations which were published and circulated by The American Assembly. Other Assemblies were scheduled to be held in Canada and throughout the United States.

The chapters which follow were prepared under the editorial supervision of John Sloan Dickey, president of Dartmouth College, as background reading for all Assemblies as well as for college and university classes and the general reading public.

As a nonpartisan educational institution, The American Assembly takes no stand on the subjects it presents for public discussion; nor is Carnegie Corporation of New York, whose generosity has made this program possible, to be associated with either the views in this volume or the recommendations of any meeting sponsored by The American Assembly.

The American Assembly

Clifford C. Nelson
President

Henry M. Wriston
Chairman

A Note on Nomenclature

In this discussion of the relations of the people called Americans with those called Canadians, what names shall we use? Who shall call whom what and in what situations? An American must be careful, in some circumstances, of calling himself so, since he may be thought to be arrogating to himself as a citizen of the United States, the name of a whole continent. Canadians are North Americans as much as he. But if he doesn't call himself American, the Canadian will; no one will call him a United States-er. The Canadian, if he be English by mother tongue and not of French descent, will think of himself as Canadian; he will call another breed French Canadians. That other breed, however, being very likely descended from the earliest settlers of land now part of Canada, will perhaps call himself *Canadien,* while he refers to the other as *Anglais,* or—with some indulgence—as *Canadien anglais.* Each kind of Canadian takes to himself the name, in his own language without an adjective. He qualifies the other. Of course we know about "Yankees" and "Canucks" and of qualifying adjectives.

The key to the problem is not the publication of a manual, but the development of sensitivity to situations. Sometimes the thing to do is to keep fencing until the other fellow names himself and you. But that does not always work, for a person does not always grant one the right to call him as he called himself. In our discussion I would suggest that we use what comes natural in the English language. We should speak of Americans and Canadians when the reference is general. As the occasion demands, let us speak of French Canadians and English Canadians. My personal rule about Americans of various kinds is to keep *American* the designating noun, while using an adjective for some other attribute: thus, Negro Americans and white Americans if there is need to make the distinction, not American Negroes and American whites.

Everett C. Hughes

Table of Contents

John Sloan Dickey 

Introduction

An Undertaking in Understanding

This book aims at a better understanding of the relations in time, place, and human affairs that add up to the phrase each of us uses with such unconscious ease: "the United States and Canada," or vice versa. Insofar as a collaborative effort of this sort can have a theme, it is that this phrase represents something more than a conglomerate of physical facts and puzzling problems—something more than those separable relations between two nations which on the organization charts of foreign offices are neatly segregated as political, economic, and cultural.

The component realities are not ignored, but our hope is that their treatment here and the discussions attendant on this book will further the realization on both sides of the border that "Canada *and* the United States" is today and will be tomorrow something more than the sum of the parts; that it is a relationship with its own individuality and its own organic integrity. For an understanding of this relationship is profoundly relevant to our modern-day "hewers of wood and drawers of water" and their counterparts in the

---

JOHN SLOAN DICKEY, *president of Dartmouth College, held positions in the Department of State in 1934-36 and in 1940-45, serving on the legal staff and as director of the Office of Public Affairs, and also with the United States delegation to the United Nations Conference on International Organization at San Francisco. Author of various articles on education, law, and foreign affairs, Dr. Dickey was a contributor to an earlier American Assembly volume,* The Secretary of State.

groves of academé and government, "hard-nosed" problem fighters.

Two difficulties have long plagued the subject. On the one hand, it is hard to get any people in the United States to take a sustained, serious interest in the subject, in part at least because unlike Africa, for example, it seems to have no mystery about it, no prospect of anything very new. On the other hand, almost anyone in either country who writes about the two countries finds himself for one reason (to attract readers) or another (to air grievances) focusing primarily on problems rather than on the significance and functioning of what Professor Hughes in the opening essay calls "the system of the two societies." We may be sure that whatever else the future brings to our understanding of "the United States and Canada," it will not and ought not bring less attention to the problems. It is a sign of maturity that the problems of the two countries increasingly are coming under sustained private study by joint groups "taking a North American approach." The twenty or so publications of the Canadian-American Committee established in 1957 by the National Planning Association (United States) and the Private Planning Association of Canada are a notable example.

To study problems, however, is not in itself to treat them, particularly for the kind of preventive therapeutics so essential to any modern social system. The kind of penetrating comparative treatment of the two societies found in S. M. Lipset's *The First New Nation* suggests that the scholarly foundations are now being laid for a more encompassing approach to this relationship. The contribution of this American Assembly book toward that larger approach will result from the cumulative impact of the six essays rather than from any common purpose of the participants. The contributing authors are allied in this project by their individual qualifications to handle assigned segments of the subject and not by any concert of concept. Although each author has, of course, been free to handle his assignment as his convictions and taste dictated, he has in the main accepted rather than created the boundaries of his segment.

Although the book has not been dominated by any prescribed point of view, the contributing authors come from both countries and, more importantly, the first four were asked to approach their assignments as scholars (and gentlemen, of course) rather than as Canadians or Americans. Let there be no doubt that this placed an unequal burden on the Canadian participants. The public climate of the two countries today burdens a Canadian scholar more heavily than his American counterpart. Even here the fact of imbalance or asymmetry is perhaps the single most pervasive characteristic of the relationship.

An awareness of the full-bodied nature of the relationship has also been sought by mustering professional specialists from sociology, history, political science, foreign affairs, economics, and literature. Each of them, in addition to his expertness, has at one time or another had significant personal experience with the other country. Acknowledging that no six individuals could hope to represent all aspects of two large countries, the professional and personal background of this group covers almost everything except full geographic distribution. This lack merely reflects practical exigencies.

The pattern of the book should speak for itself, but the objectives that dictated it ought to be mentioned. Aiming at providing the general reader with a comprehensive introduction to the relationship of the two countries, we have sought a pattern that would combine scope, concreteness and an embracing coherence, a difficult combination for any book.

The open-ended challenge to our understanding of what might be loosely termed the "human relations" of the subject comes at the outset. The societies of the two countries have had the attention of scholars, but until quite recently there has been little scholarly attention to the comparative, cross-cultural aspects of the relationship. Naturally enough politicians, journalists, and after-dinner speakers have not permitted this spacious vacuum of knowledge to remain empty of opinion. As Professor Hughes indicates in the opening chapter, there is a foundation of sociological knowledge developing, but by and large our most significant insights in this area are still essentially do-it-yourself creations. On both sides of the border we can and do "let ourselves go." Therefore both logically and practically sociological analysis makes a good starter for us.

Whether history joined the two countries as President Kennedy stated, or divided them as Professor Eayrs suggests, there is no question about its relevance to the relationship we seek to understand. It may be going a little too far to say that all one really needs to know is the history and geography, but certainly no one is going to understand very much about anything American-Canadian unless he feels at home with these exceedingly stout roots. There may be other contemporary international relationships more dominated by history and geography, but not many in which the United States has more at stake. The appropriateness of having this aspect of the book written by an American scholar, Professor Wade, will not be missed in Canada, where American indifference and ignorance to the common—or uncommon—background are legendary.

The assignment of the "hard issues" of defense, trade, and—hardest of all—independent Canadian nationhood, to the Canadian participants, particularly Professor Eayrs of Toronto's Department of Political Economy, also has a special fitness. These problems are as bilateral as problems can be (although certain of the answers may be largely unilateral or even multilateral). Qualified Americans can analyze such problems as well as their Canadian counterparts, but when it comes to sensing their part in the total relationship, one must *feel* as well as understand them. To feel the heat along with the chill there is no substitute for standing with your back to the north.

The chapter by John Holmes opens out from problems which are essentially continental to those which arise from the heavy and progressive involvement of the two nations in world affairs. At this point the fact of sharing a continent becomes subtly but definitely subordinate to the newer and larger truth that the United States and Canada must now make sense to the rest of the world as well as to each other. Here we enter the outer international dimensions of the relationship; both nations are adjusting old loyalties and assuming new obligations while faring on a modern witch's brew of real and fancied grievances, disputed dangers, competitive disagreements, the enticement of ever more ambitious solutions—all heavily seasoned with a hundred or so other unfamiliar nationalisms.

The closing chapters by Professors Viner and LePan return to the heart of the relationship, the informed understanding of individuals in the two societies. They view the outlook for the relationship as an American economist and a Canadian humanist, respectively, from personal perspectives which have involved the other country and careers which have embraced both scholarship and public duty.

A pattern of emphasis builds up as the essays variously touch the same circumstances or concern. No attempt has been made to eliminate this type of overlapping since in most instances to do so would seriously impair the basic aim and vitality of the project. Even so, as a matter of editorial judgment, certain subjects have rather arbitrarily been ruled in or out of bounds for particular chapters. For example, the exceedingly live question of "trading with the enemy" is both a bilateral "hard issue" and a problem in world affairs that bedevils NATO as well as the United States-Canadian alliance. Both to avoid duplication and to get the larger perspective, the subject is dealt with mainly in the context of the alliance.

On the other hand, each of the chapters refers to the growing role of French-Canadian "nationalism" in the relationship of the two countries. In this case any duplication is more than justified by the need to bring home to readers outside French-Canada, particularly but not exclusively Americans, the pervasive and pressing importance of this circumstance today as compared with very recent yesterdays. In January 1964, *The New York Times* did not hesitate to say editorially that it was now clear that Prime Minister Pearson's "chief problems are not foreign but domestic. . . . The chief problem . . . is what he called in his recent report to the nation the 'outburst of provincial and sectional feeling' . . . a turning point in Canadian history is approaching. . . . An exceptionally strong flare-up of racial and provincial feelings in Quebec has brought these issues to a head." *The Times* was right in characterizing this problem as primarily domestic, but it would be folly not to recognize that only a positive approach to it by all Canadians can keep it from becoming a national tragedy that could precipitate the most serious international consequences.

Along with all the asymmetries that characterize Canadian-United States relations there is a certain symmetry in their crises. At the moment Canada faces the danger of a fundamental cleavage arising from history and ethnic division, the United States has been shaken by its own domestic crisis over the issue of civil rights for its Negro citizens. Although the United States civil rights problem has not been a direct threat to the relationship of the two nations, thoughtful persons on both sides of the border recognize that anything except a positive and adequate national response could so weaken the American position in world affairs as to reveal in tragic irony the dependence of Canada on the character of American nationalism as well as on its power.

Finally, that famous border gets repeated attention throughout the book, not, I need hardly say, because it is undefended, but because, as Hughes, Viner, and Wade all emphasize, it operates so unequally as a boundary segregating two national societies. It bears repetition that the Canadian people from coast to coast live physically and mentally on the border. Whereas in sharp contrast the great majority of Americans not only do not live near the border; they are—for both better and worse—largely unmindful of it.

The pull of the border is felt in every area of Canadian life. Probably the fundamental factor in the relationship of the two countries, it can hardly be otherwise in the future. The significance of this is beyond calculation, but considering the elementary law of physics that endows every action with a reaction, it might be helpful for the role of "the unequal border" to occupy time at least equal to the "undefended border" in the oratory of the two countries.

In truth, Canada as a nation can hardly do other than *react* from the pull of an "unequal border." This poses for Canada one of the most profound predicaments of her national life. It is a predicament which is fully sensed only by those who know the national necessity for this reaction but who also know that a reactive nationalism is not enough for the kind of nationhood and independent national identity Canada seeks—and merits.

Of course, national predicaments in the relationship are not confined to Canada. American nationalism has its peculiar predicament which, as one might expect, is basically a world-wide predicament rather than one that arises primarily out of the Canadian-United States relationship. I cannot put it more vividly than by borrowing the insight Robert Frost struck on when he remarked: "How hard it is to keep from being king when it's in you and in the situation." How hard, indeed; but international kingship is harder still.

This project speaks both to national predicaments and to the underlying fundamentals, but it bespeaks no bargain-day, ready-to-wear solutions. The spirit of the book is one of a disciplined, sensitive realism which views the difficulties of the relationship as part of life's challenge to Canadians and Americans rather than as a pathological condition to be exorcised through either hostility or indifference. If the book teaches any gospel in its aim at enlarged understanding it may be that, while peevishness makes poor use of understanding, good-natured ignorance is not enough to achieve a successful relationship.

Geography, history, self-interest, the Cold War, and national emotion are realities not likely to be transformed in our time merely by more understanding; but their sum is also a reality which grows in significance with understanding. As Douglas LePan suggests in the final essay, Americans and Canadians alike will comprehend the rest of the world much better if they work a little harder at understanding the factors and forces that are fashioning their own relationship.

The understanding sought here is not a passive thing. It will only be achieved as individuals on both sides of the border test their existing attitudes by actively considering more knowledge and fresh ideas. The meetings to be sponsored in both countries by The American Assembly will stimulate this kind of thoughtful talk. We hope that readers, whether participants in these conferences or simply concerned citizens, will find themselves drawn into an open-ended dialogue.

Whatever else the reader may conclude he will not doubt that "the United States *and* Canada" gives the word "and" one of its most strenuous but also one of its most promising assignments in the modern community of nations.

Everett C. Hughes 

1

A Sociologist's View

The undiplomatic relationship

On January 11, 1964, some fifty Canadians are reported to have marched in front of the United States Consulate in Montreal to protest rough treatment of other protesting marchers by the police in the state of Georgia. The picketing of a United States office by Canadians is relatively new, but the lack of diplomacy it expresses is as old as the two countries.

The relations of the people of the Government (formerly Dominion) of Canada and the United States of America have been as notoriously undiplomatic as they have been, in a formal military sense, peaceful. That, indeed, seemed to me one of the chief findings of the study of Canadian-American relations made under the auspices of The Carnegie Endowment for International Peace in the 1930's. As I put it in a review of four volumes resulting from that study, "[The relations] have been exceedingly undiplomatic, for the contact is so close that almost any citizen of either country is ready to venture an opinion upon the affairs of the other"; I see no reason to change the statement now, except to make it stronger and to go into detail. In doing so, I shall state facts known to many

EVERETT C. HUGHES *is professor of sociology, Brandeis University. A student of Canadian affairs, he served on the faculty of McGill University from 1927 to 1938 and was an exchange professor at Laval University, 1942-43. A member of the University of Chicago faculty from 1938 to 1961, Dr. Hughes is a past president of the American Sociological Association. He is the author of* French Canada in Transition, *among other publications.*

Canadians and Americans, but to a larger proportion of Canadians than Americans, for one of the findings of nearly all studies of Canadian-American relations is that a Canadian is more apt to know the States well than an American is to know Canada well. Thus, an American writing to Americans about Canada may appear to Canadians to be writing for ignoramuses; he is also likely to display his own ignorance at some point. No American should ever write about Canada, just as no English Canadian should write about French Canada; not if he wants to come out with a whole hide. The underdog has always the sharper tongue; lacking other weapons, he needs it.

How different, how alike?

At the risk of being both obvious to Canadians, and condescending to Americans, let me go into some detail on how our countries, and the relations between them, differ from those of the classical diplomatic type. We are close to each other; how close? We are alike in language and culture. How much alike, and what is the significance of both likeness and differences? We are both new peoples and new states. How new, and to what extent do the people of each country accept the eternal existence of the other? Our boundary seems political, not cultural; is it? We are obviously not equal; Canada has the larger territory and heavens knows what hidden resources under her ice and snow; we have a ten-times larger population, more capital, bigger military establishments, and consequently greater international responsibilities.

Suppose we start with closeness. Two of the longest international boundaries in the world join the United States with the other two large countries of North America. The Mexico-United States boundary, more than 2,000 miles long, makes those countries very close indeed to each other. The penetrations of culture, people, goods, and capital across that border are, and always have been, massive and fateful. Mexico has boundaries to her south, but taken alone or together, they are as nothing in social, economic, and political importance compared to her United States boundary. The Canadian-United States boundary is even longer. It is Canada's only boundary, although polar air navigation is giving her a new border with the Soviet Union, made more tangible by the Dew-line: for the first time Canada is physically between the United States and another country. The effect is not so much to make her close to Russia as to make her proximity to the United States more acute.

Both these long boundaries, although not among those being

actively questioned at present, are the result of wars, declared and not declared, and of long conflict between people pushing on beyond "the border"—the border, that is, in the peculiar North American sense of the edge of settlement. The settlers of North America paid little attention to frontiers agreed to by treaty. As Frederick Merk shows in *Manifest Destiny and Mission in America,* the United States in effect recognized no boundaries on this continent for a long time; it was all ours to occupy, to civilize and to prosper in. Having pushed the Mexican border back to its present place (deep in what had long been Mexico), we lost our taste for "continentalism" in that direction, perhaps because we were now sure of our Pacific front and also perhaps because we had, as Merk says, "a national reluctance to add peoples of mixed blood to a blood that was pure, and an unwillingness in some parts of the population to have unfree blood added as well."

The Canadians, being of European origin and, outside Quebec, Protestant, seemed fit candidates for the blessings of our kind of democracy. We are always a bit astonished that Canadians do not want to be United States Americans. We did not quickly give up the notion of including the northern and northwestern portion of the continent within our boundaries.

Border migrations and intermingling

But the fixing of the boundary had little to do with actual migration. As Canadians and Americans moved west, they paid slight attention to boundaries. As students of migration have shown, more people make short moves than long. The Jenks', Cushings, Haights, and many others pushed across the uncertain boundary from Vermont and New Hampshire into the Eastern Townships of Quebec. The Painchauds moved down over the Quebec boundary back of the Adirondacks; one can follow them today as the name on the rural mailboxes changes letter by letter, until it becomes Pinchot in the neighborhood of Tupper Lake, a lumber town of the kind to which French Canadians gravitate in Maine, New York, upper Michigan, Oregon, Washington—and British Columbia. The French Canadians have never been border minded. A Catholic bishop of Burlington, Vermont, estimated at 500,000 the number of French Canadians in the United States in 1869. Whether he was right or not, the number of residents of that extraction was certainly much beyond a million in 1900. Being sensitized to French-Canadian surnames, I see them in pure or modified form pretty well wherever I go in the United States. Indeed, I think it likely that there are more people of French descent in the United States than in Canada.

The emigration of great numbers of rural people was, I believe, the chief reason why French Canada remained relatively unchanged as long as it did. Now that the French have swarmed to their own cities, in such number as to become more urban in residence, although perhaps not in mentality, than other Canadians, they are clamoring for change in their educational system, their constitutional arrangements, and, to some extent, the traditional leadership of their clergy. In Canada they remain an ethnic minority with a strong home base; in the United States they become assimilated, as do immigrants.

Meantime Pennsylvania Dutch (Germans), on their way west, got over into Ontario and founded Berlin, which became Kitchener in World War I. Assorted Americans, some of them not long from Scandinavia, moved north into the Prairie Provinces when that part of the country was being settled. Some of my great-uncles and uncles went to the Dakotas; one of them, during his brief career of cowpunching, got over the line. He brought back a pretty, blue-eyed, black-haired bride, an Ontario Irish Protestant girl who had gone west. Her adventures turned into the rearing of a large family of children in rural Ohio. For if people went west, many came back—on one side or another of the border. The night boat of sentimental memory brought Maritime girls to be maids in Boston houses and young men to work in the factories or go to Harvard and become famous professors, doctors, businessmen, or just common men.

Along all that long boundary short-distance movements have confused whatever tendency the border may have had to become an ethnic or linguistic frontier. Even if those who crossed stayed on the other side of the boundary from where they were born, they generally did not consider themselves emigrants and were not considered immigrants by their neighbors. In fact Americans who live in Canada are notorious for acting exactly as if they were at home, for not becoming naturalized, and even for taking it for granted that their children will remain American. Yet Raymond Brétoni, a Canadian sociologist, recently found that while immigrants from most countries form societies of their own in Montreal, Americans do not. They simply join the Canadian organizations. Some years ago there were 50,000 people of Canadian birth in Chicago; it was difficult to keep a Canadian Club going. It had to be revived periodically. Neither Canadians nor Americans act like immigrants when they cross the line. Trains, planes, and cars take people across the border in greater number than ever—in the normal course of business or pleasure, to visit relatives and friends, to go to weddings (sometimes their own), to attend universities, or to take new jobs.

Along this border there is intermingling scarcely to be found along any other. It seems a boundary that is stable and will not be moved. Yet during much of the history of the two countries there has been pressure on the boundary from one side or the other. Since Canada became a political entity, the pressure has been from the United States side. To Canadians, who feel pushed, the United States must seem very close indeed. Apart from that feeling, Canadians are indeed closer to Americans than Americans are to Canadians.

A border people

There are approximately ten Americans for every Canadian: about 190,000,000 to 19,000,000. The proportion has remained about the same for many decades. Drop them all on a flat plane and each Canadian will fall closer to the nearest American than will each American to the nearest Canadian, several times over. But we aren't distributed by chance. When at home, the average Canadian appears to live about 50 miles from the endless border. The average American lives hundreds of miles from it. One fifth of all Canadians live in Montreal and Toronto, which are almost on the border; add Vancouver, Winnipeg, Windsor and Hamilton—all close to the border—and one has caught over 5,000,000 of the Canadians—between one third and one quarter of all of them.

In Canada as in the United States, rural population is an ever smaller part of the total; only about 11 per cent of Canadians live on farms. Growth is in the cities; most of the cities are close to the border. But even the rural population hugs the border. Canada's open frontier is to the north rather than to the west. It is a chronic frontier; preaching and subsidies have failed to shift the rural population much to the north where they would be safe from baneful urban (American) influence.

Industry, especially the exploiting of ores and earths in demand in these nuclear times, takes people and activity northward; but it takes more machinery rather than people, for machinery does the work. All in all, the Canadians are probably moving closer to the border; Americans probably are not. Florida, Texas, and California, the great American population magnets, take people—some of them Canadians—farther than ever in physical distance from that peaceful border.

Canadians are the greatest telephoners on earth, with their

more than 600 calls per person per year. Americans are not far behind. The people of both countries have cars, radios, and television sets in similar proportion. I should think them likely to travel about the same distances from home. If all Canadian territory were easy to travel over, a Canadian could travel further and stay in his own country than any other car-owning national. In fact, it is the American who can and does travel farthest in his own country. The same considerations that make the Canadian live close to the border make the lines of travel run close to it. A look at any Canadian map shows that travel routes not merely run close to the border, but are inclined to dip over into the United States. Only in 1962 was the Trans-Canada highway complete. The odds are greatly in favor of the Canadian visiting the United States. Since there are ten times as many Americans as Canadians, it is many times more likely that a Canadian will take an American spouse, have American friends and associates. Mass and distance, in the absence of language barriers and with only a mildly troublesome passing of the border, conspire to make the Canadian closer to Americans as measured by contacts.

Another asymmetry of closeness and difference of size may be called the "headquarters" effect. These two countries are highly industrial, and have high standards of living. Both production and distribution are organized into a large-scale system of institutions. Given the tendency to large-scale organization one would expect the dominant centers to be in the larger part of the two-country system. And so they are, not only in the control and financing of industry and advertising, but in fashion, communications, the arts, learning and science, the professions, unions, and probably the rackets.

Learning and science

The same wave of growth of higher education is sweeping over both countries as the birth cohort of the war and postwar years comes of age and as the technological revolution reduces the demand for people of little education and increases the demand for technical training, and scientific and humane learning. The 129,000 full-time students in Canadian institutions of higher learning in 1961 were 65 per cent more than the enrollment of 1956; the estimate for 1970 is about 312,000. As in so many things, Canada falls somewhere between the United States and Britain in the proportion of her youth who go on to higher studies. The increase in enrollment is accompanied by expansion of existing institutions and by an increase in the number of colleges, universities, and post-high school vocational and technical schools. The greatest increase seems to be in Ontario, the most populous province, where there are already a number of new universities and some new colleges attached to existing universities; a total of nineteen institutions, I am told, in which one may work for a degree. This represents in part a movement of higher education out to the smaller cities and to the northern industrial towns; in part an elevation of technical and teachers' colleges to university status. A similar increase occurring in the Western provinces is so rapid that the new institutions must seek staff in the larger United States market.

Although differences between the educational systems make it hard to compare the French universities and classical colleges with the English, it is clear that there is a great expansion in higher education in French Canada as well, but that the proportion of French young people in universities is far below that of English. The new nationalists call for making French-Canadian institutions the equal of English ones in preparing people for positions of leadership in the new industrial era. A recent article in a French paper estimates that to equal the United States, French-Canadian universities would have to multiply by eight the number of doctorates given per annum.

Canadian institutions of higher learning have had more uniform standards of admission and graduation than American ones; the standards have been good, if sometimes stodgy. Some academic people fear that the great increase of students and institutions will lower standards. I think this unlikely, for the power to grant degrees is much more closely controlled than in the United States.

Although there has been a great expansion of graduate enrollment in Canada (118 per cent from 1956 to 1961), it is still relatively small compared to that in the United States. A large but unknown number of Canadians pursue graduate studies in the United States; surveys indicate that about two thirds of them take employment in Canada. The dependence of Canada on American graduate schools and research establishments is a matter of much concern in Canada. An editorial in *Le Devoir,* a leading Montreal daily, asks whether Canadians are not colonials in the matter of scientific research, since a good part of the medical research done in Canada is supported by the United States National Institutes of Health. The United States spends several times over as much for medical research per capita—and remember there are ten times as many American capita.

The editorial writer goes on to say that French Canada is even poorer in its research establishment. He might have noted the analogy with the South, where—until Texas bloomed with the black roses of oil—there were not many great fortunes and where the colleges ran to religion, letters, and law, rather than to science. Canadians who have made fortunes are great enough givers, and for the same kinds of things—universities, hospitals, churches, charities. But there are not so many Canadian fortunes; and as for great French-Canadian fortunes, is there one? The larger American foundations usually offer their grants and fellowships to Americans and Canadians, treating America north of the Rio Grande as a unit. No Canadian foundation has yet become known as a continental giver of scientific support; as far as I know, only one offers its grants on the southern side of the border.

One should note, however, that in Canada the government has long supported education, science, and the arts in a more forthright way than does the United States government. The National Research Council, the Film Board, the Canadian Broadcasting Company, and the Canada Council are government agencies which support and encourage a broad range of activities. Canadians seem not to have to think up devious reasons for such support as Americans do. Much of the liveliness of musical composition and performance, ballet and theater and the documentary movie in Canada has been due to this continuous support, given without any nonsense about making Canadians fit to fight communism.

The common market for talent

In the upper-middle range, the Canadian is probably on the average better read and more sophisticated in the arts and in international affairs than his American counterpart. Yet the finer edge of sophistication is to be found in certain centers in the United States. Certainly the headquarters in art, science, learning, is apt to lie on the southern side of the border; and the eye gets fixed on the main stage, the big tent. "We [French-Canadians] see our best men go to the English-Canadian institutions who lose theirs in turn to the Americans." How many times have I read that allegation (which was stated in a paper of January 4, 1964) in newspapers, magazines, and books and heard it in Canadian sermons, lectures, and political speeches, French and English, in the more than thirty years of my contact with Canada! It is often accompanied by complaint that the Americans have more money and buy off the talented Canadians. That is probably not the correct statement of the case. The range of positions and of incomes is probably greater in the United States; the headquarters in many lines is south of the border. The concentrations of activity are larger and absorb more people.

It is a characteristic of the industrial, urban world—perhaps more true of the United States and Canada than of any other countries—that it is a world of professionals: professional managers, engineers, accountants, scholars, scientists, doctors, lawyers, and the others, old and new. The new professionals tend to be itinerant, to get up in the world by moving about from one place of work to another. In industry and business, the tendency is to be moved about within the same large company, which has plants or offices in many places. In the academic world, the system includes many institutions, independent of one another yet in close communication. Professors get ahead by moving about, as well as by going up through the academic ranks. So do scientists, and even physicians in those specialties which are practiced in large clinics, hospitals and laboratories. Every profession or line of work has its orbits; a man may move in a small one or a large one. In the newer sort of profession, involving work in organizations and promotion by moving around, the leading orbits pay little attention to the border between the United States and Canada, except when the United States government gets worried about "security" and stops the American with a secret from leaving or a suspect Canadian from coming in.

At a given point in a man's career, the next step may often be made quicker in the larger continental market than in the smaller Canadian one. It happened to me both ways. When I was ready to take an academic post, McGill University in Canada was clearly one of the better things going for a new Ph.D. in sociology. When Chicago offered me a very modest salary eleven years later, McGill was quite willing to let me go rather than raise the ante. I'm afraid crossing the border was the least of my thoughts in either move; I suspect it is more so, but hardly an over-riding consideration, for Canadians in the same box. A Canadian, however, is more likely to be in that fix than is an American, for the reasons already given. An actor, athlete, scholar, scientist may cross the line simply to keep in a job, or to go to the top. An author may stay at home, but publish in New York.

It is hard to speak of this phenomenon without getting into very hot water, for one appears to be judging quality. It is not that. The headquarters institutions usually have exaggerated opinions about their monopoly of quality. We all know the professor who made his name in some midwestern state university, or a Canadian one, but grew his paunch in New England. We are speaking of systems of institutions, with a common market for personnel of certain kinds. Some are nearer the apex in reputation, money, and power than are others. That apex, in factors involving both countries, is more likely to be in the United States even though average quality may be better in Canada and the lowest of the low may be in the United States. Given the very great similarity of our cultures and institutions, a common market for talent is inevitable. Given the disparities of size and distance, the movement is bound to be more in one direction than in the other. It is also bound to be a matter of greater concern to Canadians; it is one of the things which gives Canadians, in some measure, a sense of being a minority. The poor French Canadians are a minority within a minority (and a very good thing for this great agglomeration of car-driving, telephoning, TV-baseball-football-movie-watching, do-it-yourself English-speaking North Americans to have in their midst).

Whether a Canadian professional man (including the itinerant professional business executive) actually crosses the line for a job or not, he will have connections over the line. He will belong to trade associations, scientific, professional, or learned societies. Very likely, if he is, say, a hospital administrator, he will belong to a provincial or country-wide Canadian organization (if there isn't one for hospital administrators in most provinces, a French one, and one for all of Canada, there soon will be). If he moves in a larger orbit, he will also belong to a larger association, probably called American, which has its headquarters in the United States and generally meets in the United States. The American of the same profession will belong to a state, perhaps a regional, and certainly the "American" association. If the Canadian is the publishing kind of man, he will sometimes publish in the Canadian organ of his trade; but sometimes, unless his specialty is distinctly Canadian, he will seek to have his work published in the "American" journal, with a continental circulation. I find that the articles which I have published in Canadian journals are less known to my American colleagues than those which appeared in American periodicals. My Canadian colleagues, who live in the "Provinces," know both their own journals and those of the larger world.

Let me hasten to put the record straight on Canadian science and scholarship. Canadian scholars and scientists have their own problems to work upon and have always worked upon them. As in the United States, private institutions of higher learning were established early in the East; as one goes west, provincial (state) institutions predominate. The chronology of settlement and of establishment of institutions of learning is about the same except that when one gets west of Ontario it is generally later in Canada. Scholars and scientists who work on peculiarly Canadian matter tend to stay in Canada. A considerable portion of those who work on more universal matter start and finish their careers in Canada as well. There is a lively itineracy in all professions within Canada itself, and there are many scholarly journals of quality. Canadian learned societies meet in the charm and informality of their university campuses, not as in the United States in great hotels. I go to the Canadian Political Science Association meetings not merely to see friends, but also to refresh my memory of what sociological meetings used to be like in the United States (when we were fewer and poorer).

The myopia of ethnocentrism

This is the point at which to say something about Canada and the United States in general. A feature of ethnocentrism in a large country is that its people find it hard to understand that a much smaller country is just as mature, viable, well-established, and distinct as the larger. Add to this the relatively small overt differences of culture and language, and one gets a situation in which the larger is inclined to assume that the smaller is an accident which will soon fade away. English Canadians seem to assume that French Canada will go away, that it won't always be French. Americans seem to imply, by many words and deeds, that Canada will not always be Canada. Every people likes to believe itself eternal. Neither kind of Canadian, nor the American, can pretend that their people existed, as a distinct group, from the beginning of time. But we can argue about who got here first. The French Canadians can do pretty well on that argument, speaking as a "national" group. The United States can do better than English Canada, and can point to a considerably earlier establishment of an independent state. But some Canadians can get around that by saying their ancestors lived in the American colonies, but were of more aristocratic origins than the Franklins and Adams' and elected to remain true to King George III. Thus there are in both countries people who claim peculiar merit because of their ancestors: the United Empire Loyalists in Canada, whose merit it is to be descended from people who fought the ancestors of the Daughters of the American Revolution. They are incidentally quite indistinguishable from each other, and should by all rights arrange for joint membership, not merely on the grounds of the likeness of their place in and views of the world, but because in many cases their many eighteenth-century ancestors include some of both sides. (Typically, my Canadian wife is eligible by descent for both, not to mention any organization of people of French-Canadian descent. I, typically, have no ancestors who ran off to Canada during the Revolution. They ran off to the mountains instead.)

There is a certain strain between the two countries over the matter of time past and time future—about our age, and about our duration. French Canadians are the oldest group in our triangle; the United States is the older independent political entity and the largest. But the English Canadians, too, opened up country and set up government. Indeed, they say that they are the true carriers and practitioners of Anglo-Saxon responsible government on this continent, while yielding to no one in independence from outside controls. Yet Americans find it hard to feel in their bones that a Canadian is as Canadian as an American is American, and needs take no more thought (although he does) to be so; the English Canadian for his part, finds it hard to believe that a French Canadian is French Canadian simply because he was born so, and not for any contrived reason, although of course, being under pressure, he does contrive a reason.

The overseas input

Our two peoples are modern mixes, blended from European overseas migrations which began in the seventeenth century and still continue, and later migrations from other continents. The United States got fewer of the early French migrants, but it is not at all unlikely that there are as many people of some French ancestry in the United States now as in Canada, although they have no strong centers of culture and have largely lost their identity. The United States generally got more British immigrants than did Canada year by year, until very recent times, but they are less in evidence in the larger country.

On the frontier of both countries, as that frontier moved west, religious sects sought to establish their peculiar kingdoms of God in peaceful isolation from the World: Mennonites, Hutterites, Doukhobors, Latter Day Saints. The world always caught up with them, tempting the saints to follow the world and attacking them if they did not. The United States, with large territories suitable for plantation agriculture, had a larger part in the forced migration of Africans to America—thus making her social structure in the Southern regions resemble that of the West Indies and some parts of Latin America. Westward migration and expansion, with military force, gave the United States a considerable dark-skinned, Spanish-speaking population, which Canada does not have.

Trans-Pacific migration provided Chinese and Japanese laborers for construction and agriculture on the western coast and in the western mountains of both countries, together with communities of active small entrepreneurs in the coastal cities. Recent migration from Europe is probably of about the same composition in both countries but the United States continues to get, in addition, large numbers of Latin-Americans, poor, unskilled, and of little schooling.

The minorities

Although a large proportion of the two peoples are of about the same mix, the largest minority of each country is quite different from that of the other. Obviously the two great minorities are the French in Canada and the Negroes in the United States. In one respect, the two are alike; both are native. Find that part of any large American city in which 90 per cent of the population is native-born of native-born parents; it is a Negro district. Find it in Canada: it is French. Although much of the talk and thinking about such matters in both countries assumes that minorities are immigrant, unassimilated immigrant minorities are no longer a problem in either country. The immigrants of yesterday are part of the majority which today deals with the large native minority.

The United States literally created its own minority. White Americans brought Africans to serve as plantation labor, bred with them, and so organized the lives of the progeny that they lost the culture of their African ancestors without having full access to Euro-American culture. They were given, in practice and in law, a special status far out of keeping with the principles of equality written into the American Constitution. The members of the resulting minority, similar in number to the total population of Canada, still suffer from the poverty, lack of schooling and skills, physical peril, and personal insult and humiliation visited upon them a century after their nominal emancipation from slavery. They are engaged in a massive struggle to remove the distinction of status, in law and in practice. They ask that the concept *Negro* disappear from American law and custom. But other Americans have not yet allowed the special status of Negro to disappear. Some wouldn't mind, providing the Negroes were at a distance. A few join in the struggle. A large and concentrated group fight the change so bitterly as to change the very course of government.

Canada's great minority, the French, antedates the creation of a Canadian government. It is a classical territorial, linguistic, and cultural minority, a self-conscious, stubborn group of people whose ancestors got there first and sent down deep roots. They seek to maintain an historic special status. Many of them insist that there is not a Canadian people, but two peoples, or nations, bound into one state by an agreement which they do not consider sacred or immortal.

However much may be made of differences in our cultural liturgy which I shall mention later, I doubt whether they are of great importance in the relations between Canadians and Americans. The deeper misunderstandings probably come from strains which, in turn, are caused by the different situations in which we find ourselves and the different internal problems which we have to meet. Of the different internal problems, perhaps the most important is that more than a third of all Canadians are of a cultural and linguistic minority demanding its rights in one way, while twenty million Americans are of a racial minority demanding their rights in quite a different way. The tone, the rhetoric of internal politics, is different because of these two great internal problems. It is the stress and strain of meeting problems that makes our relations what they are, not merely our very similar culture and history.

Contrasting constitutional crises

Thus both these countries are involved in fundamental constitutional debate aroused and colored by the struggle over the status of the large minority in each country. The debate brings out some perhaps rather fundamental differences. In the modern nation state one is supposed to believe that his immortal people has now got its just dues, a state which will also be imperishable. The notion that any state can be of tentative constitution, and probably not immortal, is political heresy; especially where there is no sacred, symbolic monarch. Americans are especially absolute in their ideas on this point.

Canadians generally are probably less absolute in their notions about nations and constitutions, within which changes can be made. But English Canadians often seem to regard French Canadians as a group which will, or ought to, disappear into the "Canadian people," which they think of as having a long, if not eternal, future.

Many French Canadians think of the present constitution of Canada as a contract, a *mariage de convenance*—probably not so contracted as to come under the Church's protection as a valid marriage—subject to renegotiation when no longer *convenable.* I believe that these differences of view about the nature of the constitution often confuse communication between Americans and Canadians.

During the war I sometimes went out to talk to American audiences about Canada's war effort. On more than one occasion my companion, a Canadian official, blamed the French Canadians for the fact that Canada did not send drafted men overseas. The Americans who had raised the question clearly implied something like this: "What kind of country is it that can't draft its people if it wants to? The French are Canadian citizens, aren't they? Canada is in a war, isn't it?" The poor Canadian, who knew very well that large numbers of Canadians, French and English, were serving abroad before the United States was in the war still thought he had to apologize for the lack of a drafted overseas army. This story illustrates what I mean by the absolutism of American political philosophy, and a certain greater flexibility of Canadian. The minute we got into the war, our way was the right way. The Canadians should follow it. The official who accompanied me on these excursions was driven to the common defense of accusing some one else. The Americans, with a divine assurance that they are right, feel quite free to ask the Canadians, "why don't you do as we do?"; that is, as we have been doing since yesterday noon. There is a certain pressure of American criticism on Canada, especially with respect to such matters as Cuba, the Cold War, and China. Forty years ago, it was prohibition. Canadians, I think, feel that they must excuse the fact that they do not follow American policy and actions. Perhaps their ambivalence about the United States and Americans comes partly from the fact that they have, on so many points, similar sentiments and might come to similar decisions, yet being independent and acting separately, they do not come to identical and simultaneous decisions. There is nothing so infuriating as to have the detail and timing of one's actions dictated, or urgently proposed by some one else who has no more commitment to the ideal or cause than oneself. Again the French Canadians are a minority within a minority. The English Canadian sometimes comes stiffly to attention and tells the French their duty. The French like neither coming to attention, nor being told their duty. They would rather do their duty in secret than to have it thought they were doing it because they had been told.

It's not that Canadians would not gladly, and do not, tell Americans their faults and their duty. But Americans are so numerous and far off from Canadians; they simply don't listen, and hence bear no malice.

But if some of the features of ethnic composition of the two populations (and the two or three peoples) appear to make both internal relations and the relations between the two countries more difficult, they also make them closer and more harmonious. Most special kinds of Americans—by religion, race, national origin, occupation, or other identifying traits—have their counterparts with similar problems in Canada. Hearty athletic Irish priests have to deal with their Latin counterparts in both countries. Mormons in Alberta are of the same community as those in Utah and have similar neighbors to contend with. Beyond that, however, the people of each country can use some of their fellow-countrymen as scapegoats for their own sins and failures. Thus are we drawn together in uneasy peace, a *pax familias.*

Cultural liturgies and attitudes

Thus far I have woven what I have had to say about the relations of the two countries into a web of structure and ecological relations. I have done so because I think the conscious attitudes, such as are uttered in opinion surveys, of the people of the one country toward those of the other cannot be understood without keeping these ecological relations in mind. It is customary to say that Canadians and Americans are annoyed with each other because they are so alike that any deviation of either from their common culture is regarded as sacrilege by the other. That reaction does, indeed, occur. Battles rage over the "or" as against the "our" ending of words, and over small or large differences of pronunciation. This is not to be wondered at in the particular case, although it is one of the more fantastic of human phenomena. Alphabets, spelling, pronunciation, vocabulary are the stuff of which nationalist movements are made; at least, much is made of them in such movements. Poor Canada is caught between England and the United States in this, as in many other matters, such as the handling of knives and forks. On the whole, it is the Canadian who has deep feelings on these matters, probably just because of being in the cross fire between Mother Britain and Uncle Sam.

But we must speak of "attitudes." Canadians have attitudes about almost everything American; Americans are not well enough informed to have so many about Canada. Canadians participate in the World Series of baseball and the American presidential election; at least, the talking and betting at the McGill Faculty Club used to be concentrated on those events at the appropriate season (and not by my initiative or that of other Americans). Canadian papers are full of news from the United States; Canadians talk about the American news of business, of sports, scandal, and whatever else is stirring. Attitudes are expressed, but they are generally not explicitly "attitudes about" Americans and things American.

Of course, there are such attitudes. Some English Canadians are bitter about the United States and about Americans; it is a deep, dark bitterness and dislike, expressed in a waspish way. It does not turn up in the polls of opinion, so far as I have seen them. I have no idea how widespread it is. But it exists, and there is no use pretending it does not. So far as I know, it never caused me, an American, to be kept out of a house or a party; but one never knows that sort of thing. An elderly cousin of my wife's did introduce me thus at a tea a few weeks after my arrival in Canada: "This is my niece's husband. He's an American. But you would never know it!" She was drawing me into the inner circle of kin and friends, not reflecting on Americans. She was of that convent-bred generation of Montreal and Quebec women, French and English, who thought that they lived at the center of the world beyond which lay the outer darkness. Another cousin of the same kind kept asking me for ten years when I would finish my course "up at the college." An American could only be at McGill to take a course! Such provincialism is to be found, I suppose, wherever there is a local in-bred society with strong sense of class and family. Americans, being outside that system, were odd. One could be kind to them, as to other people one had never heard of.

The prevailing stereotype is of another kind. As Professor S. D. Clark, now of the University of Toronto, reported it in a study based on interviews with English-speaking Protestants in Montreal in the 1930's, the American is boastful, excitable, materialistic, inclined to law-breaking and divorce, and very ignorant of Canada. One finds them hospitable and perhaps agreeable, taken individually, but one can't take them in a group. A good many exceptions were made for people one knew well. Canadians who live in cities, and especially those near the border are apt to be influenced by American ways, especially the bad ones. In fact, as I reread Clark's report on *Canada and her Great Neighbor* (1938) I am reminded—as I was at the time—of the way my rural Ohio relatives talk about people from New York and Hollywood, and about how the young people who went bad did it under the baneful influence of those centers of sin.

Since the studies of the 1930's the techniques of surveying opinion have been refined—and more money is available for them. Raymond Bréton, a young Canadian sociologist who has been reviewing the polls, notes as a first significant point that Canadians are never asked about the influence of England, France, or Europe as a whole on Canadian life; they are asked only about the United States. The United States is the constant, inevitable point of comparison.

In a 1961 study of a representative sample of people in the cities of Montreal and Quebec, only 21 per cent were found to agree with the proposition that "the immorality which we observe in Quebec is often due to the evil influence of the Americans"; 62 per cent did not agree. In the province outside the cities only 25 per cent agreed, while 54 per cent did not agree. In a general Canadian poll people have been asked in several years whether they think the Canadian way of life is too much influenced by the United States. They have answered thus:

	1951	*1956*	*1957*	*1961*
Too much	30	27	21	38
Not too much	48	63	57	49
No opinion	16	10	22	13

In the 1961 poll, 23 per cent thought, for example, that "We copy the Americans in our way of life; they are faster living; more materialistic." From the figures it appears that a good solid core of Canadians continue to have about the same opinions that Clark found twenty-five years or more ago. But it is a minority countered by a larger percentage who say they do not hold those views. It also appears that the percentage fluctuates rather widely. It would be interesting to know with what conditions and events the opinions rise and fall, for the actual influence of Americans and their actual character, however volatile, can scarcely vacillate so rapidly. No doubt economic conditions and political events affect these opinions.

Opinion as to whether eonomic control is a good thing or not also fluctuates. In 1956, nearly 70 per cent of people questioned in all regions of Canada thought it a good thing that "a lot of Canada's development has been financed by United States money." In 1963, the percentage had dropped to about 55 throughout the country. Even the percentage of Canadians who believe Canada is becoming more dependent on the United States fluctuates somewhat, although it is more stable than the other opinions we have noted. One Canadian, whom I do not have the right to quote at present, believes that the instability of Canadian opinion about the United States may come from a certain feeling that their own Canadian actions are without great significance, a feeling which may breed a certain alienation which is expressed in negative attitudes. I repeat his idea because it suggests that the matter is one that is not completely understood and should be probed. As more and more countries become industrialized with capital from the great central industrial countries, similar situations and attitudes may occur in many parts of the world. In the poll figures which I have seen, there are no correlations of attitudes toward American economic control with judgments of American people and morals. One would expect such correlations. In our civilization morality and economics are considered strongly connected in people's judgments.

Aggression by communications

This is also a world in which people read newspapers and magazines, listen to radio and watch television. Control of these media and the content of their messages is considered very important in determining behavior. Canadians have always been great consumers of "mass communications"—to use the awkward common phrase—from the American side of the line. And it worries them. I sensed this when I first crossed that border. In fact, when I went to Vancouver in 1927 to "speak to father," he gave me quite a talk about how in Canada they were a little more restrained and modest in advertising than in the United States, and about how the press was not so sensational. As he was talking he was showing me through Vancouver, the Canadian Pacific railway yards and docks, the gateway to the Orient. In the yards stood an express car with a great banner on it: "The First Carload of Kotex to Cross Canada." That, of course, though embarrassing, illustrated the point; Kotex and the advertising of it were American inventions.

When I first went to live in Montreal I thought it would be interesting to see what parts of Canada preferred United States popular magazines to Canadian and those from England. It was a naïve notion, but I learned much by trying it out. The city of Victoria on Vancouver Island turned out to have the highest circulation per capita of the Canadian *MacLean's Magazine, The Saturday Evening Post,* and also of a couple of popular English weeklies. The circulations moved up and down together. In some parts of Canada people simply read more magazines of all kinds. The circulation of magazines from England was quite small; *The Saturday Evening Post*'s circulations were of the same order of magnitude as in American cities. As for Victoria, when people weren't looking after their roses, they had to have something to do. As another index of American influence I took divorce rates. The rates in the Canadian Provinces were much lower than in the various States, but as one went west the rate went up: the peak was on the west coast in both countries. Magazine circulation also went up as one went west, but Ontario (with much the largest urban English-speaking population) stood high on these measures of "Americanism."

Canada has met the "problem" of American publications in various ways. There have been attempts to control the amount of advertising by United States businesses, to require Canadian advertising and to "clean up" the content of what comes in. The protection of Canadian business from an excess of United States advertising is, of course, one of the strong motives for discouraging circulation of American magazines. *Time* magazine years ago established a Canadian edition to meet the requirements; its Canadian circulation was apparently large enough to warrant it. Other magazines have not done so; as far as I know there has been no decline of the reading of United States magazines. But the Canadian *MacLean's Magazine* has prospered so greatly that it has established a French edition, the only English-Canadian publication to do so.

The penetration of Canada by American communications has been made more massive by radio and television. Not only are a large proportion of all Canadians within easy tuning reach of American stations; the Canadian stations also run many programs of American origin. In the control of radio and television, Canada lies somewhere between Britain and the United States. Commercials are less blatant, long, and frequent than on the United States radio and television. From the early time of radio, the Canadian Broadcasting Company, a government agency, has owned stations and run programs. Until the burgeoning of FM stations, there was nothing in the United States to compare with the CBC programs for quality and for relief from interruption by silly ditties, commercials spoken in various kinds of affected voices, and generally unpleasant noises and talk. A greater measure of control was also exerted over the private stations in Canada than in the United States.

The Canadian Broadcasting Company has recently made a survey of opinions of its listeners. Nearly all the respondents thought nearly all the stated goals of the CBC were important: to encourage Canadian talent, to educate, tell the news and entertain the people, and to help Canadians understand each other. Very few people thought too many performers were hired from the United States; indeed, a larger number thought more should be hired. A fifth of all respondents thought that even their own CBC-run programs for children are harmful to them, and 24 per cent that too many of the plays show the seamy side of life; yet only 12 per cent believe that many CBC programs have a bad influence on people's morals. Those who think things are bad tend to be rural, English, elderly, and Bible Protestants—like Americans of similar opinions about radio and television. No doubt those same people would think independent and United States radio and television programs even worse.

Whatever some Canadians may think of United States programs, a very large number of Canadians hear and view them in a big way. In November 1963 three Buffalo affiliates of United States networks took 43 per cent of the total viewing audience during peak evening hours in Toronto: United States stations, presumably those of Seattle, took 37 per cent of the Vancouver audience in the same period. In addition many popular United States programs are carried on both independent Canadian and CBC stations. It is reported that Canadians absolutely loved the fourth Nixon-Kennedy debate, which was presented on CBC-TV. Apparently Canadian viewers simply take to the programs which they can enjoy, without much thought about their origins. Origin is mentioned by the audience mainly when they are for some reason annoyed.

Yet there are differences between those Canadians who say they prefer CBC stations and those who prefer independent Canadian and United States stations. Among those who prefer the CBC stations are distinctly more people who have been to university, who are in professional occupations, and who are older. Among those who prefer the other stations are distinctly more young people and workers, from skilled to unskilled. It seems clear that there is a substantial group of people whose preference for the CBC is marked. From my own experience, and from listening to comments of Americans who have heard CBC programs, I believe that there is a group in the United States who would like programs such as those of the CBC, and that this group is very like the Canadians who like the CBC. Paul Gardner wrote a piece along these lines in *The New York Times* of January 19, 1964. He spoke mainly of the quality of the drama done on CBC, and of the opportunity for actors to develop professionally on CBC-TV as they cannot on United States television, with its guest appearances and star system. American visitors to Canada find CBC discussion of international affairs much more free of attempts to justify government policy than on the supposedly private stations in the United States. It may be that Canadians are just annoyed enough by United States attempts to keep the media in line to insist on their freedom of discussion. The main effect of having government-supported radio and television in Canada has certainly not been bias in political news or discussions; nor has it been neglect of popular taste. It has been a determined, if moderate, attention to other tastes, so that more time is given to plays, intellectual programs, and good music. To achieve this end in an American city requires a committee of public-minded citizens with money, university people, and people engaged in the arts; they must carry on a campaign in competition with other philanthropies, and generally must avoid programs of political significance.

In radio and television, as in other matters, we are dealing with a continental system in which the Canadian part cannot be understood without the rest. It might be hard to show that the Canadian part has any great influence on the rest. At least one may speculate that the presence of such an independent system (to reverse the terms as generally used by suggesting that the government-owned Canadian Broadcasting Company stations are more independent than privately-owned stations in the United States) may check some of the extremes of American communications, and may give an example which can be followed and material which can be used.

The neglected study: the integrity of the system

In conclusion, it is important to keep in mind that these two complicated urban industrial countries are part of a common system, that each is deeply dependent upon the other, and that they are bound by kinship, economy, organization, tastes, standard of living, and many common problems. One cannot describe either country without taking the other greatly into account. It is, however, amazing how little the two countries have been studied as parts of a system. One studies a system not by showing the likenesses and differences between its parts, as in classifying butterflies on pins, but by analyzing the functions of each part for the others and for the whole.

The chapters which follow seek this kind of understanding of the United States-Canada relationship.

Mason Wade 

2

The Roots of the Relationship

Canada and the United States have been aptly described by the foremost student of their relationship, the late J. B. Brebner, as "the Siamese Twins of North America who cannot separate and live." Although the unique relationship between the two countries cannot be explained wholly in North American terms—for both are involved with Great Britain in what Brebner christened the "North Atlantic Triangle"—its basic roots in a largely common geographical environment and in a partly common history cannot be ignored, for they are the very essence of the relationship.

Geography and history still affect in countless ways the interplay between the two countries, to an extent much better appreciated by Canadians than Americans. Canadians have long sought to create artificial east-west ties to offset the powerful pull of the natural north-south ones, and their history is largely one of conscious effort to resist being engulfed by their much more populous and powerful neighbor, while maintaining closer ties with it than exist between any other two nations in the world. Canada has been called "America's problem," but the United States has many prob-

---

MASON WADE *is professor of history and director of the Canadian Studies Program at the University of Rochester. He is an American who has served at length in Canada in both academic and diplomatic capacities and has written five books on Canadian subjects. Professor Wade is vice president of the Canadian Historical Association and chairman of the American section of the Joint Committee of the American and Canadian Historical Associations.*

lems which loom as large or larger; for Canada the United States is *the* problem.

The Geography of a Shared Continent

The interplay between the two regions began soon after the continent took form and geological revolutions reared up the mountain ramparts on its eastern and western shores. Canada and the United States share the Appalachians and the Rockies, but Canada alone has felt the effect of a third, still earlier convulsion of the earth which created the Canadian Shield, the huge, largely barren rock formation which surrounds Hudson Bay and forms the northern and eastern two thirds of Canada. The Shield swings down from the Arctic Archipelago east of the Mackenzie Delta to western Lake Superior, skirts Lake Huron and Georgian Bay, cuts across Ontario to the St. Lawrence at Kingston, retreats to the Ottawa River, and then runs northeast to the St. Lawrence just below Quebec City. It constitutes the forbidding shore of all mainland Canada from Quebec northward along the Labrador coast to Baffin Island—a grim coast which Jacques Cartier aptly called "the land God gave to Cain." It divides eastern and western Canada by a thousand miles of rugged wilderness, and long deflected the expanding population of the St. Lawrence Valley into the rich lands of the American Middle West. The Shield is perhaps the single most important physical fact about Canada, for it explains why Canada, with an area one quarter larger than that of the United States, has only one tenth as large a population.

The first export of resources

The Shield is also a grim monument to the first and greatest contribution of Canadian natural resources to the United States, for glaciers repeatedly pressing down from the Arctic crushed and scoured the Shield and left most of its soil in the north-central United States. Canada was not stripped wholly bare by glaciation, but its share of fertile soil was limited to pockets in the Maritime Provinces, to a narrow band on the south shore of the lower St. Lawrence (which above Quebec City broadens along both shores to include most of southern Quebec and Ontario), and to a broad expanse stretching westward and northward from Winnipeg to Dawson Creek. Elsewhere, except for isolated pockets in the Shield (such as the Lake St. John area of eastern Quebec and the Clay Belt which cuts across the Quebec-Ontario boundary south of James Bay), the soil is thin or lacking. The battered, broken plateau of the Shield, cut by innumerable lakes, streams, marshes, and muskeg, was destined to remain the domain of the fur trader and the lumberman until its unsuspected mineral resources were discovered toward the end of the nineteenth century. Then it was found that its southern extension into northern Minnesota contained rich deposits of iron, the Mesabi Range, which were far more accessible and easily worked than the Canadian deposits recently exploited at Steep Rock (1944) and on the Quebec-Labrador boundary (1954).

The area which was to become the United States also was blessed with much the best of the four great natural entrances to the interior of the continent from the Atlantic. Hudson Strait and Hudson Bay, from their discovery early in the seventeenth century, have permitted seagoing vessels to reach the center of the continent and to tap the drainage basin of one quarter of North America. But even with the most modern aids to navigation this route is practicable only three months of the year and has never realized the high hopes of its discoverers and stubborn supporters. The second Canadian entrance, the St. Lawrence-Great Lakes waterway, provided a far better route from the Atlantic to the heart of the continent, but its mouth, lying far to the north, is blocked by ice four months of the year, and its upper course was barred by countless natural obstacles which the Seaway (1959) has only recently conquered to permit ocean-going ships to proceed from Montreal to the Upper Lakes. The two American entrances, the Hudson-Mohawk route to the Great Lakes and the Mississippi system which provided access to a million and a quarter square miles of the interior, offered year-round ports and far fewer natural obstacles. In the rivalry between the St. Lawrence and the Hudson-Mohawk routes, which has continued from colonial days to the present, the natural odds greatly favored the Americans. By the end of the French regime in Canada in 1760 the Mississippi had already begun to tap successfully the fur trade of the Great Lakes which had been developed from the St. Lawrence. On the Pacific coast, which Canadians and Americans reached almost simultaneously, the former soon had to yield the disputed mouth of the Columbia River, the only practicable entry, and retreat to the almost impassable Fraser and the unsatisfactory Skeena. Though ice and cold severely handicap the Canadian entrances in high latitudes, most Canadians and Americans living in the northern United States enjoy a similar climate.

The pull of the border

Three quarters of the population of Canada live within two hundred miles of the international boundary; two thirds live south of the 49th parallel in the densely populated urban and industrial border region extending from Windsor, Ontario, to Quebec City, which includes the two largest metropolitan areas, Montreal and Toronto. The two next largest, Vancouver and Winnipeg, also lie close to the border. On both sides of the boundary the northwest is warmer than the northeast, and the midcontinent is colder in winter and hotter in summer than the coastal areas. Halifax and Boston, Toronto and Detroit, Vancouver and Seattle, have similar climates. But there is a vast inequality of natural advantages north and south of the boundary area. Canada has no equivalent of the rich Atlantic tidewater area, no semi-tropical Florida, Southwest, or Southern California; no vast corn, winter wheat, and cotton belts extending from the Atlantic piedmont to the Gulf of Mexico. The rich spring wheat area of the Great Plains west of the Mississippi and Lake Winnipeg is almost equally divided between the two countries, as are the valuable rain forests of the Pacific Coast. This varying natural endowment largely explains the difference in development between the two countries since Europeans first began to penetrate the North American continent along the Atlantic coast from Newfoundland to Florida in the sixteenth century.

The History of a Divided Continent

The white man: trade and trouble

When Europeans established contact with the aboriginal inhabitants of North America, they found them engaged in tribal wars which had arrayed the scattered Algonquian peoples of the northeast against the closely united Iroquoian tribes who were expanding north and east from their original home south of the Great Lakes. In the Arctic regions, too, there was another continuing conflict between the Eskimos and the northern Indians. The Europeans became involved in these continental conflicts, even before the French established themselves at Port Royal in 1605 and at Quebec in 1608, the English at Jamestown in 1607 and at Plymouth in 1620. For the European fishermen who frequented the Grand Banks and the Gulf of St. Lawrence long before any settlements were made gave the Indians they encountered the advantage of European goods, which were things of great price to savages not far advanced beyond the Stone Age. The Indians of the coastal regions became middlemen, exchanging European goods for the furs gathered by the interior tribes and much desired by the white men. They soon sought the aid of their trading partners in war. In 1609 Champlain accompanied the Algonquins and their Huron allies on a war party against the Iroquois. In a battle fought near Ticonderoga Champlain unwittingly opened a French conflict with the Iroquois, which made these most belligerent of the eastern tribes firm allies first of the Dutch and then of the English. From the latter the Iroquois obtained European arms, as did the Algonquins from the French. Trade rivalry strengthened the savage instinct for warfare, and white men soon shocked the Indians by playing the old game of war more ruthlessly by trying to exterminate rather than merely raid their foes.

Fur and flags fly

French and English fur traders soon came into conflict in the Acadian region. Champlain's exploring parties along the New England coast suffered reprisals which the Indians of those parts intended for the English traders who had mistreated them. Samuel Argall of Virginia wiped out the French establishments on the Maine and Nova Scotian coasts in 1613, and thus began the Anglo-French wars which continued for another century and a half. From the shores of the Bay of Fundy the commercial conflict spread northward and westward, as competition for the fisheries and the rich furs of the interior heightened the desire of the European rivals to monopolize the trade of the continent. In 1615 Champlain took part in a Huron-Algonquin expedition against the Onondaga Iroquois, who were threatening the Huron monopoly of the Great Lakes fur trade. As early as 1627 the English drafted their first grand design to drive the French from North America. In the two following years the Kirke brothers captured Tadoussac and Quebec and established Scottish colonies at Port Royal and on Cape Breton. But Acadia and Canada were handed back to France in 1632, and the English flag did not finally fly over Port Royal until 1710 and over Quebec until 1759, despite major expeditions against both places in 1690 and 1710-11. The Anglo-French conflict continued on a broad front extending from Acadia to Hudson Bay and Louisiana, even when peace prevailed in Europe between England and France, for colonial interests were often in conflict when imperial ones were not.

But there was another side to the tangled tale of colonial relations, for intercolonial trade showed a persistent tendency to develop in flat defiance of the mercantilist theories of both mother countries. In 1650 the Jesuit Gabriel Druillettes came to Boston from Quebec, offering free trade in return for an alliance against the Iroquois whose raids were threatening the life of the French colony. The rival French fur traders of Acadia sought aid from Boston in their quarrels, with a blithe disregard of imperial and religious differences. With the establishment of Louisbourg on Cape Breton in 1720 to guard the French line of communications after the loss of peninsular Nova Scotia, this French Gibraltar of the North Atlantic became an entrepôt for trade with New England as well as with the French West Indies. Common colonial interests in trade had a way of overriding imperial rivalry, and the natural north-south channels of trade sometimes prevailed over the official east-west ones. French and English war parties periodically raided each other's frontier settlements to maintain prestige with the Indians and to discourage intercolonial traffic, but furs from the French hinterland persisted in finding their way to Albany and Philadelphia, while the cheaper and superior English trade goods were frequently used by French traders. In opening the trade of the Hudson Bay region the *coureurs de bois,* Radisson and Groseillers, shifted from French to British masters and back again as the flexible Latours had done in Acadia. Even the fiery Governor Dongan of New York, who thought it intolerable that "all landes a Frenchman walks over in America must be French," found it convenient to wink at clandestine trade between Albany and Montreal. More than one French governor-general and most French commanders of posts profited from illegal trade.

A continental economy persisted in evolving despite the growing imperial conflict. Colonial commercial motives played a considerable part in such nominally imperial expeditions as Phipps's against Port Royal and Quebec in 1690 and Pepperrell's against Louisbourg in 1745, and basically determined the expulsion of the Acadians in 1755. The religious differences between Protestant English and Catholic French were exploited to create warlike enthusiasm among colonials reluctant to risk their lives for imperial causes. Even though the elder Pitt finally saw that European wars might be won on American battlefields, and then supplied the powerful imperial forces which had been lacking in the earlier North American encounters, it was the growing conviction of English North Americans that the French must be finally crushed that played the decisive part in the final conquest of the French empire in North America. The teeming seaboard colonies could then expand beyond the thinly held French frontier that stretched in a great arc from Louisbourg to New Orleans.

A bitter legacy

This American Hundred Years' War left a legacy of bitterness which still persists today among the French Canadians, and it is involved in the general Canadian resistance to American influences. The French Canadians, abandoned by their mother country to the mercy of their traditional enemies, developed a state-of-siege mentality and a preoccupation with survival which is still vigorous today. They have been encouraged by their nationalist historians to regard the heyday of New France as their golden age, which was shattered by the British Conquest. They are reminded that they are a conquered people and that the "English," whether English-Canadian or American, are hereditary enemies who still seek to anglicize and Protestantize them. (The British government vainly and briefly attempted to do this after 1763, before it granted them the guarantees of French and Catholic survival in the Quebec Act of 1774.)

The British government hoped to integrate Quebec with the other American colonies, but the old regional conflict persisted in commercial form after the Conquest. The Scottish and English fur traders from Albany and New England who took over the Montreal trade from the French inherited the French tradition of aggressive competition with the London-based monopolists of the Hudson's Bay Company and with the trans-Alleghany traders of Pennsylvania, Virginia, and Carolina. The Montrealers, backed by British capital, carried on a resourceful rearguard action against the westward march of settlement which brought them to the shores of the Pacific before they were forced to amalgamate with the Hudson's Bay Company in 1821. The Canadian fur traders then made common cause against the American traders and settlers who finally drove them to their last stand in the Canadian Northwest.

"Children of divorced parents"

The old colonial military conflict was also resumed soon after the Conquest when the rebellious American colonies tried to make Quebec and Nova Scotia the Fourteenth and Fifteenth Colonies. Although the threat to Nova Scotia proved not very serious in the face of British seapower, it created great alarm in a sparsely settled colony chiefly populated by recent American immigrants and newly returned Acadians whose loyalty was understandably suspected. But the Nova Scotia Yankees for the most part adopted the same neutral attitude as the Acadians had before them, while the latter showed some zeal against those who had been harsh taskmasters in their days of exile. The American invasion of Quebec in 1775-76 was a far more serious affair. It finally failed only after the original easy capture of the Champlain and Richelieu forts and Montreal, and the disappointing decision of most French Canadians to remain neutral in an English family quarrel. A bungled assault on Quebec and General Winter's ravages among the besiegers paved the way for a bloodless British victory when spring unlocked the St. Lawrence and brought a British fleet to relieve the beleaguered garrison. But the idea of the military conquest of Canada was revived by the French alliance and kept alive during the rest of the Revolution. The experience of invasion and occupation gave the Canadians an increasing determination to remain themselves and not make common cause with the Americans. The aftermath of the American Revolution, the forced migration of some 30-40,000 American Loyalists to Nova Scotia and Quebec, really marked the establishment of a new British North America, a divided group of colonies united chiefly by their determination to remain British and by their resentment and suspicion of their rebellious neighbors. A leading modern Canadian historian, A. R. M. Lower, has noted that Canadians are children of divorced parents, and this concept is helpful in understanding ambivalent Canadian attitudes about the United States which persist today.

The American Revolution was followed by much wrangling between the separated brethren and mutual charges of bad faith which increased the bitterness of the parting. Until 1796 Britain kept the strategic chain of frontier trading posts, stretching from Lake Champlain to Mackinac, which it had agreed to surrender under the peace treaty, as security for American compensation to the Loyalists for their losses, which the weak federal government was unable to induce the states to grant. Then, though Americans were sharply divided in their sympathies as the great conflict between Britain and revolutionary and Napoleonic France developed, French republican representatives found a warm enough American welcome for their plans of recapturing Canada to create anti-American as well as anti-French panic in Canada.

The result of an inconclusive war

The outbreak of the War of 1812, with its repeated American efforts to conquer Canada by force of arms, cemented the Canadian nationalism which had been born during the American Revolution.

This time French Canadians as well as English Canadians fought to defend their homes against the ill-disciplined American invaders, although Lower Canada (Quebec) showed much the same determination as New England to sit out the war and continue business as usual. The Canadian part of the war was fought primarily in Upper Canada (Ontario) and on the Great Lakes. Once more the forces of continentalism were defeated in a seesaw struggle. Since few British regulars could be spared from Europe to fight in Canada until the closing stages, the outcome could be credited to Canadian valor, though a more judicial view might hold that American military incompetence deserved quite as much credit. The war was inconclusive, in that the peace settlement provided for a return to the prewar status quo; but it was decisive in making clear that the division of the northern part of the continent was to be permanent, if Canadians had their way. The burning of York (Toronto), for which the subsequent burning of Washington was a reprisal, and the devastation of the Niagara Peninsula and the Thames Valley by American invaders, added new scores to the Loyalist heritage of anti-American bitterness.

But out of the war also came a series of settlements of Canadian-American issues which promised a better relationship in the future. Jay's Treaty of 1794 had invoked the principle of good neighborhood in the settlement of post-Revolution disputes; it recognized the right of Americans and Canadians and Indians freely to pass and repass from one country to the other—a right which was to persist until 1930; it established reciprocally equalized customs duties. Most important of all, it inaugurated the use of arbitration in the settlement of international disputes, which became the standard procedure for the determination of Canadian-American issues. The Treaty of Ghent of 1814, which ended the war two weeks before Jackson's victory at New Orleans, referred the vexed questions of boundaries, fisheries, and control of the Great Lakes to arbitration by joint commissions. Out of the work of these commissions came the Rush-Bagot Agreement of 1817 for naval disarmament on the Great Lakes and the Convention of 1818, which established certain perpetual rights for American fishermen in British North Atlantic waters, extended the boundary westward along the 49th parallel to the Rockies, and provided for joint occupation of the Oregon country from northern California to the southern tip of the Alaska Panhandle. Another commission reached agreement on the division of the islands in Passamaquoddy Bay, but the attempt to settle the interior Maine-New Brunswick boundary broke down in 1822. Final determination of the northeastern boundary was only achieved by the Webster-Ashburton Treaty of 1842, after a long series of border frictions culminating in the so-called Aroostook War, less gloriously known as the War of Pork and Beans.

That post-prandial favorite

There is a hardy and persistent myth that the tradition of the undefended frontier, that favorite topic of after-dinner orators, goes back to the Rush-Bagot Agreement, which dealt solely with naval armaments on the Great Lakes. In fact, two generations of rumors of war after 1815 saw the most intensive period of fortification of the Canadian border, until the Treaty of Washington of 1871 settled the outstanding differences between the North American neighbors. Though the Duke of Wellington held that Canada could not be defended against attack from the United States, the British government constructed a series of formidable works. To circumvent American attacks on the channel of communications between Montreal and Kingston—the exposed international section of the St. Lawrence—locks were built on the Ottawa River after 1819, and the Rideau Canal was constructed between 1826 and 1832 to link Ottawa with Kingston. This interior line of communications, built at the cost of a million pounds to the British taxpayer, now is a favored route of international yachtsmen, while Fort Henry, the massive citidel at Kingston built between 1832 and 1836 to guard the entrance of the canal and the naval dockyard, has become a leading attraction for American tourists. In 1819 work was begun on a new fort at Isle-aux-Noix on the Richelieu, and the Citadel at Quebec was built between 1820 and 1831, supplemented in 1865-72 by three forts at Lévis on the south shore. The Citadel at Halifax was also built in the 1830's. While from 1816 to 1829 Congress appropriated over $8 million for fortifications, most of the money was spent on coastal defenses and only about $200,000 was spent on the Canadian border, at Fort Niagara and Rouses Point. Work was halted at the latter place on what became known as "Fort Blunder" in 1818, when it was discovered that the new fortification had been built on Canadian soil because of a faulty drawing of the 45th parallel. In 1839 the Niagara and Oswego forts were renovated, and after 1841 Fort Wayne was built at Detroit and Fort Porter at Buffalo. In 1844 work was resumed at Rouses Point on Fort Montgomery, which the United States was allowed to keep under the Webster-Ashburton Treaty, and ended only after the Civil War, which had caused further fortification of Oswego, Niagara, and

Detroit as well. With the withdrawal of British troops from Canada in 1871, except for garrisons at the imperial naval stations at Halifax and Esquimalt on the Atlantic and Pacific coasts, the border was at last effectively demilitarized in the dawn of a new era of Canadian-American cooperation. But massive works along the border remain as reminders of a day when renewed Canadian-American conflict was a very present and recurrent danger, not an unthinkable eventuality.

War had been close in 1837-38, when refugees from the Canadian rebellions found American sympathizers from Detroit to Vermont; again in 1839 when Maine and New Brunswick lumbermen clashed in the Aroostook country; in 1846 in the Oregon country; and in 1859, when Captain George Pickett, later to win fame at Gettysburg, seized San Juan Island. Nevertheless, cooler heads prevailed on both sides and prevented these border "troublutions" from developing into full-fledged conflicts. It was significant of the changing Canadian-American relationship that General Winfield Scott, who won his rank for gallantry at Chippewa and Lundy's Lane in 1814, was the American emissary who preserved the peace in three of these four periods of tension. Despite his nickname of "Old Fuss and Feathers" Scott was a man of excellent judgment and common sense, whose command of the arts of peace may have exceeded his military competence.

Although Canadian sympathies originally favored the North in the Civil War, American demands for retaliation upon Canada for British friendliness to the Southern cause changed matters. In fact, Canadian hospitality to the Confederate leaders of the St. Albans and Johnson's Island raids led to a militant Northern attitude which made Henry Adams write: "The prospect of Sherman marching down the St. Lawrence and Farragut sailing up it, doesn't just seem agreeable." The Fenian Brotherhood found many willing recruits among discharged Irish-American soldiers for its effort to right Ireland's ancient wrongs by an attack upon Canada in 1866. But those who cheerfully sang the Fenian marching song,

> Many battles we have won, along with the boys in blue,
> And we'll go and capture Canada, for we've nothing else to do,

found British North Americans singularly unwilling to be conquered as proxy Englishmen. Though the border was disturbed by Fenian raids from 1864 to 1871 from Maine to Manitoba, the Fenians' sole triumph was at Ridgeway on the Niagara Peninsula in 1866, a shortlived one which ended in their arrest by the United

States authorities as they retreated across the Niagara River to Buffalo. The tenderness of state and federal authorities, mindful of the Irish vote, to Fenian violations of the American neutrality laws, led Governor-General Monck sarcastically to thank the United States government "for vigorously and faithfully putting their laws into force against the Fenians after the invasion of Canada had taken place," and increased the Canadian heritage of ill will toward its neighbors.

From annexation to a premature reciprocity

If armed aggression aimed at Canada from the United States ceased with the petering out of the Fenian raids in the face of a much stiffer attitude of the American authorities, the old American expansionist notion persisted that it was "Manifest Destiny" that some day the Stars and Stripes should wave over all North America from Panama to the North Pole. While the cry of "54-40 or fight," raised by James K. Polk in the campaign of 1844, died with his ready acceptance of the British offer of 1846 to extend the boundary along the 49th parallel to the coast and thence through the Strait of Juan de Fuca to the Pacific, there remained many Americans willing to foster the growth of annexationist sentiment in British North America. Just as New Yorkers and Vermonters had befriended the exiles of 1837 in their efforts to establish republics of Upper and Lower Canada, there were many Americans who welcomed the Montreal annexationist movement of 1849. The remedy to the establishment of free trade by Britain was to be found "in a friendly and peaceful separation from British connexion, and a union upon equitable terms with the great North American confederacy of sovereign states." The signers of this manifesto quickly found that they had gone too far in their desperation at the prospect of commercial ruin, and they turned instead to favoring reciprocal free trade in natural products between British North America and the United States.

The leading advocates of reciprocity were William Hamilton Merritt, the American-born promoter of the Welland Canal, who in 1848 as a Canadian cabinet minister presented the case for free trade to Congress; his protégé, T. C. Keefer, an engineer who helped build the Erie, Welland, and Ottawa canals and in 1851 was surveying a route for the proposed Grand Trunk Railway from Chicago across Canada and Maine to Portland; and Israel DeWolfe Andrews who served as United States Consul at Saint John, New Brunswick, from 1843 onward and as special agent of the State and Treasury Departments after 1849 to work for free trade with the

British North American Provinces. All three men were continentalists, fascinated by the economic opportunities presented as expanding canal and railroad systems opened up the Canadian-American area. Keefer's maps accompanying Andrews' official reports omitted boundary lines, and the latter argued that geography had made British North America and the United States a single economic unit. While Merritt convinced Lord Elgin, the Governor-General, that reciprocity was the only alternative to annexation, Andrews lobbied vigorously for the same cause on both sides of the border with the aid of large funds supplied by the United States, Canadian, and British governments. He was a fine early example of the American lobbyist, and his enthusiastic efforts among legislators, journalists, and businessmen probably had more to do with the passage of the Reciprocity Treaty in 1854 than Lord Elgin's judicious dining and wining of senators and congressmen in the final stages.

New England's traditional desire for free access to the North Atlantic fisheries and the Lake States' desire to use the St. Lawrence waterway as a competitive rival to the Erie Canal combined to break down the growing American tendency to establish a high tariff barrier against British North American products. As the sectional conflict between North and South became more acute, somehow the North was persuaded that reciprocity was only a prelude to the annexation of new free states, while the South was persuaded that reciprocity would prevent this result by giving the British provinces the economic basis of independence. The 1854 treaty was to last for a minimum of ten years, after which either party could give a year's notice of termination. But long before the original term was out, protectionism revived on both sides of the border, while the Civil War embittered Canadian-American relations. In January 1865 Congress instructed the President to give notice of termination of the treaty, as part of its program of reprisals which had originally included termination of the Rush-Bagot Agreement and the establishment of rigid passport regulations on the border. These measures were dropped after four months, but Canadian efforts to secure renewal of reciprocity in 1866 were rebuffed, and not until 1911 was the United States really eager to establish reciprocity once more.

"Manifest Destiny" and Canadian Confederation

The vastly more powerful United States which emerged from the Civil War was in a mood to take over the whole continent in fulfillment of the doctrine of "Manifest Destiny." Secretary of State

W. H. Seward, long a firm believer in the inevitability of the annexation of the British provinces, told a Boston audience in 1867 that "Nature designs that this whole continent, not merely these thirty-six states, shall be, sooner or later, within the magic circle of the American Union." His acquisition of Alaska that same year, and his encouragement of the purchase of the Hudson's Bay Company by an American banker, were designed to hasten what seemed to him inevitable. To Seward and many others British North America was a ripe fruit which in due course must fall into the waiting hands of the United States. Though Seward refrained from giving open support to the St. Paul expansionists who saw the uneasy Red River colony and the whole Canadian Northwest, then under Hudson's Bay Company rule, as their natural hinterland, other leading American politicians of the day were less cautious. Senator Zachariah Chandler of Michigan and Representative N. P. Banks, chairman of the Foreign Affairs Committee, sponsored a bill in July 1866 which provided for the admission of the British provinces into the Union upon request. Senator Charles Sumner of Massachusetts proposed in 1869 that Great Britain should turn over to the United States her North American colonies in payment of the *Alabama* claims. President Grant openly favored Sumner's proposal, but Secretary of State Hamilton Fish realized that, although Britain was willing to let her colonies go if they so desired, she would not cede them in satisfaction of any claim upon herself.

Fear of a hostile United States was indeed a principal cause of the Confederation of the British North American provinces as the Dominion of Canada in 1867. While only the provinces of Canada, New Brunswick, and Nova Scotia joined at first, the Confederation scheme provided for the inclusion of the others and the purchase of the vast territory of the Hudson's Bay Company, thus establishing a nation stretching from sea to sea which might hope in time to rival its giant neighbor on more equal terms. The new Province of Manitoba was created in 1870; after the collapse of the Red River Colony's revolt against Canadian rule. Lured by the promise of a transcontinental railroad and facing the same threat from American expansionism as the Red River colony had done, British Columbia joined Confederation the following year. Reluctant Prince Edward Island followed suit in 1873. Only Newfoundland persisted in maintaining her ties with Britain instead of North America until 1949.

Americans were convinced that Confederation had only been brought about in defiance of public opinion, and that when British pressure in support of it was removed and environmental factors were allowed full play, the ripe fruit would promptly fall. President Grant's reference to "the colonial authority known as the Dominion of Canada . . . this semi-independent but irresponsible agent [which] has exercised its powers in an unfriendly way" was long to be echoed in the State Department's attitude toward Canada. The Treaty of Washington (1871) settled most Canadian-American questions for the time being, referring many of them once more to arbitration, but it was regarded by Americans as an Anglo-American settlement whose conclusion had been irritatingly delayed by the stubborn reluctance of Sir John A. Macdonald, the Canadian Prime Minister, to let Anglo-American accord be reached at considerable cost to Canada. The steady development of Canadian nationhood under the long administrations of Macdonald (1867-73, 1878-91) and Sir Wilfrid Laurier (1896-1911) went largely unrecognized in a greater nation which was growing far more rapidly. Although Canadians became increasingly interested in dealing directly with Washington, the State Department continued to negotiate with Britain on Canadian matters, and Canadian interests frequently suffered in the interest of Anglo-American accord.

As Canadian-American tensions bred by the Civil War relaxed, a new reciprocity agreement was reached in 1874, only to be rejected by the protectionist U. S. Senate. In the face of repeated American rebuffs and in the midst of a world-wide depression which weighed heavily upon the young Canadian nation until 1896, protectionist sentiment grew increasingly strong in central Canada. Macdonald was able to regain office in 1878 on a program of economic and political nationalism, known as the National Policy. A substantially increased tariff was designed to assert Canada's independence of both Britain and the United States. The Pacific railroad was pushed through to completion on Canadian soil in 1885, and a program of western settlement was launched. The nation that had been envisaged at Confederation at last began to take form. But the Manitoba and British Columbia booms quickly collapsed, and the economic burden of a transportation system which as yet did not yield the anticipated benefits proved heavy. The Canadian standard of living fell below the American, and European immigrants to Canada soon moved on to the United States, following native sons who had left home in search of greater economic opportunities. The total emigration from Canada to the United States between 1881 and 1891 amounted to over a million, when Canada's total population was less than five million.

Commercial Union rejected

Disappointment with Canada's economic growth also provided fertile soil in the 1880's for the Commercial Union movement advocated by Erastus Wiman of New York, a Canadian-born financier with interests in Canadian telegraphs; his associate Samuel J. Ritchie of Akron, an American interested in Ontario railroads and the Sudbury nickel-copper deposits; and Wharton Barker of Philadelphia, another financier. Congressman Hezekiah Butterworth of Ohio made himself the spokesman of Commercial Union in Congress, calling for the mutual abolition of customs duties, the establishment of a common tariff, and the division of its income between the two countries. Wiman launched an active publicity campaign in both countries, which was supported by the president of the Toronto Board of Trade, two leading Toronto newspapers, and Goldwin Smith, the former Oxford don who saw Canada's only future as part of the United States.

Commercial Union found favor with some Liberals, notably Sir Richard Cartwright, the party's financial expert, though it was repudiated by the successive Liberal leaders Edward Blake and Wilfrid Laurier. The latter favored instead Unrestricted Reciprocity, which called for free trade between the two countries without assimilation of the Canadian and American tariffs. After the adoption of the high McKinley tariff in 1890, reciprocity became the major issue of the 1891 Canadian elections. Macdonald, rebuffed in his attempt to secure free trade in natural products, denounced reciprocity as "veiled treason which attempts by sordid means and mercenary proffers to lure our people from their allegiance." Macdonald made telling use on the platform of a stolen private pamphlet written by Edward Farrer, editorial writer for the Toronto *Globe,* which suggested means by which the United States could encourage the annexation of Canada. He was able to exploit the rising tide of imperialist feeling in Canada by proclaiming "A British subject I was born, a British subject I will die" and rallying his followers to the cry of "the old man, the old flag, and the old policy."

The dawn of "Canada's Century"

Commercial Union and Unrestricted Reciprocity both became firmly tainted with annexationism, and when the Liberals finally came to power in 1896 and were confronted with the still higher Dingley tariff in the United States, they adopted instead a moderate protective tariff which contained the germ of imperial preference. The Joint Commission of 1898-9 was unable to reach any agreement on reciprocity or any other of the Canadian-American issues considered. But it was now Canada which opposed reciprocity, for its transcontinental economy was finally becoming profitable, with Britain almost twice as important a customer as the United States. Laurier could justly observe that "the general feeling in Canada today is not in favor of reciprocity," and announce that "there will be no more pilgrimages to Washington."

An increasingly prosperous Canada, whose population between 1901 and 1911 for the first time grew faster that that of the United States and which attracted over a million settlers from the United States between 1897 and 1914, tended to assert its independence of both Britain and the United States in the years before World War I. Canadians enthusiastically agreed with Laurier that the twentieth century was to be Canada's century, as the nineteenth had been that of the United States. The coming of a million British immigrants after 1896 strengthened Canada's ties with Britain, but Canada's leaders deftly evaded British efforts to link her more closely with the mother country by formal political, economic, or military arrangements. American protectionism and aggressive imperialism, culminating in President Theodore Roosevelt's high-handed determination in 1903 "to run the [Alaska Boundary] line as we claim it without any further regard to the attitude of England and Canada," led Laurier to voice in Parliament his regret that Canada's neighbors were "very grasping in their national actions and . . . determined on every occasion to get the best in any agreement which they make." Significantly, Laurier went on to regret Canada's colonial status and to announce her determination henceforward to manage her own foreign affairs. Canadians generally interpreted the unfavorable Alaska Boundary Award as a sacrifice of their interests on the altar of Anglo-American understanding, and this episode greatly strengthened the Canadian nationalism which had been slowly growing since Confederation.

The lingering bitterness left by Roosevelt's big-stick tactics in the Alaska matter paved the way for an explosion of Canadian nationalism in 1911, when Canadian public opinion overwhelmingly rejected the reciprocity agreement which had been worked out between the Taft and Laurier administrations. Canadian manufacturers and railroads combined their formidable forces to defend their own interests against those of the reciprocity-minded West. They were greatly aided in their all-out effort "to bust the damn thing," in the classic phrase of Sir William Van Horne, the American-born former head of the Canadian Pacific Railway, by some incautious utterances of American public men. President Taft's reference to Canada being "at the parting of the ways" and Speaker Champ Clark's declaration, "I am for it, because I hope to see the day when the American flag will float over every square foot of the British North American possessions clear to the North Pole," led Canadians to interpret reciprocity as but a preliminary to annexation. In defeating the proposal Canadians clearly enjoyed telling the Americans that they could get along without them, despite the increasing integration of the Canadian and American economies brought about by growing American reliance on Canadian raw materials and on the Canadian market, which had become the third most important for the United States.

Despite these stormy episodes which strengthened the tradition of anti-Americanism, some real advances were made in the Canadian-American relationship between 1903 and 1911, thanks largely to the determined efforts of Secretary of State Elihu Root and British Ambassador James Bryce to heal the wounds left by the Alaska Boundary Award. In 1909 the Boundary Waters Treaty crowned the exploratory work of the Joint International Waterways Commission since 1902. It established a code of principles to govern the use of waters shared by both countries, and it set up a permanent International Joint Commission with equal representation, to decide judicially and on technical grounds whatever problems were pending or might arise between the two countries. The IJC was designed to settle without the cumbersome procedures of diplomatic negotiation the host of problems which constantly arose as a result of the geographical and economic relationship of the two countries. It was a unique institution, devised to solve the problems of a unique relationship, and it provided the precedent for the creation, during World War II and since then, of a host of joint bodies modeled upon it. It established the Canadian-American tradition of settling matters at issue by private discussions around a table on a basis of equal representation, rather than in the political arena where the vast differences in power between the two countries could be invoked.

Another achievement was the settlement of the legal aspects of the long vexed North Atlantic fisheries by reference to the Permanent Court of Arbitration at The Hague, which handed down its judgments in 1910. Further disputes over fisheries inevitably arose, but they became less acute as new technical methods eliminated the basis of many old quarrels. A mutual interest in conservation tended to replace the old rivalry, although the competing interests of the Maritime and New England fishermen in the American market, and the extension after 1949 of fishing privileges on the Atlantic banks to other nations in accordance with traditional Newfoundland practice, aggravated old or raised new problems.

Common Causes and the Common Defense

The growth of the North American relationship

Despite her symbolic declarations of independence from Britain and the United States, the outbreak of World War I demonstrated Canada's continued integration in the North Atlantic triangle which had arisen from the interlocking of the American, British, and Canadian economies. Canada offered Britain her aid before the formal declaration of war, and as her economic war effort outstripped even her remarkable military contribution, she turned to the United States for much of the capital that made possible the vast expansion of Canadian industry. American investment in Canada, which by 1914 had already reached a total of $700 million, nearly doubled by 1920, while British investment remained constant and then began to decline from its 1914 total of $2,000 million. Canadian imports from and exports to the United States both more than doubled between 1914 and 1918, in which year it was estimated that American investors owned 30 per cent of all Canadian industry. An irreversible integration of the Canadian and American economies took place, as North America became both the granary and the arsenal of Britain and France. After 1918 the influx of American capital continued to mount, reaching a total of $2.5 billion—$300 million more than all other foreign holdings combined—by 1924, and over $3 billion by 1928. The establishment of Canadian branch plants by American industry to profit by the British preference was an important aspect of the immediate postwar period; by 1925 it was estimated that there were over 700 wholly-owned branch plants and at least 900 more partially or completely controlled by American capital.

A more independent Canada

This American economic penetration provided fertile soil for a Canadian nationalism which had grown greatly during the war. It had asserted itself against Britain in Sir Robert Borden's successful effort to secure for Canada a voice in the Imperial War Cabinet and separate representation at the Peace Conference. Canadian official susceptibilities were ruffled by the evident reluctance of the United States to accept Canada's role at the Peace Conference and her separate membership in the League of Nations. Canadian private susceptibilities were even more violently irritated by the freely expressed American conviction that the Americans had won the war. American neutrality until 1917, and increasing American prosperity during these years when Canadians were experiencing a spartan wartime economy, nourished a deep and lasting antipathy that was made more bitter by the contrast between Canada's losses in nearly four years of fighting and American losses during ten months in the field. Canadians never forgot that with one thirteenth of the American population they had suffered two thirds as many casualties. For Americans the war began in 1917, while Canadians who had been engaged since 1914 tended to forget how much the American entry contributed to the faltering Allied cause and to the final victory. Although there was a remarkable official and private coordination of the war efforts of the two countries after April 1917, and President Wilson's idealistic plans for the postwar settlement aroused great enthusiasm in Canada, old prejudices were revived in the postwar years when the American workers of the eleventh hour seemed to be taking over the Canadian vineyard. American repudiation of the League of Nations contributed to Canadian bitterness, although as time went on Canada lapsed more and more into the same North American isolationism displayed by the United States.

Canada's new North American orientation was evidenced by Mackenzie King's resistance after 1921, on the basis of anticipated American objections, to all British efforts to involve her in imperial responsibilities. As early as 1918 Borden had warned the Imperial War Cabinet that Canada would not support any policy directed against the United States, and at the Imperial Conference of 1921 Arthur Meighen successfully opposed the renewal of the Anglo-Japanese Alliance which appeared as a naval threat to the United States. He thus paved the way for the Washington Armament Conference which halted the world-wide naval armament race and redressed the balance of power in the Pacific.

The Balfour Declaration of 1926, which became law in the Statute of Westminster (1931), provided formal recognition of the independence of Britain which Canada had in fact long been exercising. In 1920 Canada had made provision for separate representation at Washington, and in 1923 she had insisted on negotiating and signing the Halibut Treaty with the United States on her own. In November 1926 Vincent Massey was appointed as the first Canadian minister to Washington, and in February 1927 William Phillips was named as the first American minister to Ottawa. The long existing interplay between the two nations and the new importance of each to the other was recognized by the establishment of a direct diplomatic relationship. In its announcement of the appointment of Mr. Phillips, a high-ranking career diplomat, the State Department noted that "our relations with Canada are of vital importance to both countries." Canadian recognition of this fact was implicit in the sending to Washington of Canada's first diplomatic representative. It had already become clear that Canada was moving out of the British orbit and into the American one.

Smoot-Hawleyism and the Ottawa Agreements

Canada's new continental orientation was briefly reversed when the 1929 crash revived the forces of American economic nationalism and produced the Smoot-Hawley Tariff of 1931 which raised rates on Canadian raw materials to prohibitive levels. R. B. Bennett, the pugnaciously protectionist Conservative who turned the Liberals out of office in 1930 on a platform of "Canada First, then the Empire," countered with a high tariff against American goods, and finally persuaded a reluctant British government to adopt his imperial preference scheme which resulted in the Ottawa Agreements of 1932, raising still higher the tariff wall around the Commonwealth countries. The effect of this tariff war was to reduce Canadian trade with the United States by 1933 to 31 per cent of its 1929 level, and unanticipatedly to increase the incentive to establish American branch plants in Canada when North America began to emerge from the depths of the depression. The economic isolationism dominant in both countries was also reflected in 1930 by close restrictions on the free movement of people back and forth across the border which had characterized the relationship since Jay's Treaty. From 1930 to 1936 some 100,000 Canadians returned home from the United States, but this was an insignificant reduction of the 1930 total of 3.3 million of Canadian birth or parentage who were then living in the United States, one quarter of the total Canadian stock in North America.

New deals in trade and politics

The election of Franklin D. Roosevelt to the presidency in 1932 and the subsequent introduction of the New Deal had widespread effects in Canada, for American efforts to restore the economy were both felt and copied in Canada. The arch-Conservative Bennett, strongly influenced by his brother-in-law, W. D. Herridge, the Canadian Minister in Washington who was close to the President, was finally induced to launch in 1935 a Canadian New Deal closely modeled on the American one. Bennett had not been enthusiastic about the reciprocal trade policy introduced by Cordell Hull in 1934, but Mackenzie King, upon his return to office in October 1935, promptly concluded a trade treaty with the United States that did much to free Canadian-American trade of the restrictions which had been increased from 1930 onward. After the Ottawa Agreements terminated in 1937, it was possible the following year to make new treaties between the three members of the North Atlantic triangle which applied the pattern of reciprocal advantage on a much broader basis.

This economic rapprochement was paralleled in the political field. President Roosevelt, as a former governor of New York and a summer resident of Campobello Island, New Brunswick, had a real interest in Canada. His application of the Good Neighbor policy to that country was no mere formality. He was a strong advocate of the St. Lawrence Waterway project, which Congress had refused to ratify in 1932 and which he revived again in 1938 and 1941, despite widespread opposition in both countries. His state visit to Canada in July 1936 revived a Harvard acquaintance with Mackenzie King which was to have important implications for Canadian-American cooperation in World War II, when the Canadian leader often felt closer to Roosevelt than to Churchill. At this time King showed no public interest in American overtures for Canadian cooperation in the maintenance of peace in the Americas, though he doubtless derived assurance from Roosevelt's observation at Chautauqua that August that the United States was prepared, if need be, to defend its neighborhood against aggression. The two leaders had private discussions before the President made this assurance specific when receiving an honorary degree at Queen's University at Kingston on August 18, 1938: "The Dominion of Canada is part of the sisterhood of the British Empire. I give to you assurance that the people of the United States will not stand idly by if domination of Canadian soil is threatened by any other Empire." Two days later at Woodbridge, Ontario, King cautiously welcomed Roosevelt's statement, describing it as one made with no thought of a military alliance, but recognizing that Canadians had their own responsibility to see to it that "should the occasion ever arrive, enemy forces should not be able to pursue their way, either by land, sea, or air, to the United States across Canadian territory." The Prime Minister took pains to stress that there was no weakening of Canada's ties with other members of the British Commonwealth. But implicit in this exchange between the American and Canadian leaders was a new emphasis on Canada's position as a North American nation, which resulted in secret staff discussions of common defense measures in the event of attack.

Partners in war and the common defense

The ground was thus well prepared at both the political and military top levels for the Ogdensburg Agreement of August 18, 1940, announcing the creation of a Permanent Joint Board on Defense (PJBD) to "consider in the broad sense the defense of the north half of the Western Hemisphere." While the fall of France and the virtual destruction of the British Army in June undoubtedly precipitated the formation of a new North American alliance, King noted that it was no temporary expedient, but "part of the enduring foundation of a new order, based on friendship and goodwill." It was a new order indeed for the Canadian military establishment, which as late as 1920 had envisaged its main problem as the defense of Canada against invasion by the United States. Some subsequent wartime irritations might have been avoided if the American forces serving in Canada had been more historically aware of such traditional Canadian attitudes.

But as Winston Churchill told the British Parliament two days later, forewarning it of the destroyers-bases agreement with the United States, the English-speaking democracies had to become "somewhat mixed up together in some of their affairs for mutual and general advantage." The PJBD held its first meeting in Ottawa on August 26, later meeting monthly alternately in Montreal and New York. It discussed such vital projects as the defense of Newfoundland, the construction of the Alaska Highway, the Northwest Staging Route, the Canol project, and the establishment of American weather stations in the Canadian Arctic to facilitate the ferrying of planes to Britain by way of Iceland and Greenland. Despite persistent Canadian fears that the American "occupation" of the Canadian Northwest might prove to be permanent, the military installations there were turned over to Canada at the end of the war. But the development of intercontinental air warfare and the emergence of the missile threat later made it clear (as was agreed, February 1947) that henceforward continental defense would have to be closely coordinated in time of peace, as well as war.

The Hyde Park Agreement of April 1941 between Roosevelt and King provided for a coordination of the economic effort of the two countries and relieved Canada of an approaching shortage of American dollars. Although Canada itself received no assistance under the Lend-Lease Act of March, Canadian purchases in the United States which were to be embodied in equipment and munitions for Great Britain, did come under the American arrangement with Britain.

From these two major agreements for the coordination of the military and economic war efforts of the two countries developed a closely knit cooperation. Canadians and Americans served together in many outposts. The Canadian and American economies were virtually integrated. This joint North American effort produced a spectacular development of Canadian industry and agriculture, while American investment in Canada rose from $4.1 billion in 1939 to $5.1 billion in 1946. Canada became a major industrial power, which emerged from the war, like the United States, unscathed and far stronger. But it had become dangerously dependent upon the United States, while its prewar markets outside of North America were largely closed by the postwar sterling crisis. For these reasons Canada immediately launched a determined effort to develop a more multilateral economy, just as it sought relief through the multilateral relationships of the U.N. and NATO from its subordinate role in its bilateral relationship with the United States.

World War II immeasurably strengthened Canada's close ties with the United States which geography and history had long determined, but it also greatly strengthened the Canadian determination to maintain a separate identity, to be North American with a difference characterized by emphasis on its dual French and British heritage, and its separateness from, if not its equality with, the United States. Canada has always been a willed nation, existing despite the conscious and unconscious forces which have sought to absorb it into its much more populous and powerful neighbor. As the postwar period opened, the will to maintain the Canadian nation which had achieved new world status as a result of its remarkable wartime efforts was probably stronger than ever before, and continuing boom instead of anticipated depression revived the hope of the twentieth being Canada's century. A Canadian nationalism which had long reacted against British dominance was now to react chiefly against the United States, as Washington replaced London as the chief center of influences upon Canada, and as American pressures on Canada increased in countless ways. But coupled with the instinctive traditional tendency to resist Americanization was the reluctant realization that, whether Canadians liked it or not, Canada's destiny was now bound up with that of the United States, that the north-south continental relationship had become immensely more significant than the traditional transatlantic ones. As the North American relationship became closer and more complex, inevitably there would be still greater need for the mutual tolerance and recognition of the interdependence which had overcome the old antipathies still lurking beneath the cordial surface of the relationship, in Canada if not in the United States: antipathies which unhappily could still be revived upon occasion.

James Eayrs 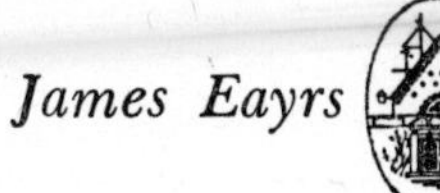

3

Sharing a Continent

The Hard Issues

The Politics of Neighbourhood

When newly independent nations enter the world arena for the first time, they tend to regard themselves as being above and beyond the struggle for power. The cynical aphorisms of the worldly philosophers—Kautilya's definition of your enemy as that State which is on your border and of your friend as that State which is on the border of the State which is on your border; or Hobbes's depiction of nations "in continual jealousies, and in the state and posture of gladiators"—do not, they think, apply to them. Not for them, either, the sordid maneuvers of older countries. The young, if they keep their principles (and their distance) may remain immune to the aches and agues afflicting the established members of the states-system. The pursuit of allies, the mollification of neutrals, the accumulation of arms, the imposition of boycott and embargo, the entire ritual of that fevered, frenetic statecraft Machiavelli aptly called *combinazione*—from all this they are exempt. They may indeed hope for more than mere exemption. For if, in their relations

---

James Eayrs *is professor of political economy, University of Toronto, and co-editor of the "International Journal." He has written extensively on Canadian foreign affairs. Among his publications are* The Art of the Possible; Northern Approaches: Canada and the Search for Peace; The Commonwealth and Suez; *and* In Defense of Canada, *Vol. I (forthcoming).*

with one another, their fraternity and good neighbourliness glow with a kindly light through the encircling gloom of the international anarchy, it may lead others to emulate their example. They have a civilizing mission.

Canada and the United States, though not newly independent by the standards of Upper Volta and the Malagasay Republic, are young enough by the standards of Greece and Rome. While they may look back, respectively, upon a century and three centuries of national history, it is only within the last generation or so that they have been impelled to leave the cocoon of North American isolation for the wilder shores of international politics. One may therefore expect to find in the outlook of each something of the characteristic outlook of new-found independence. One does find it.

World War I which brought so many North Americans to Europe, brought Europe no closer to North America. The trauma of the trenches produced in both Canada and the United States the conviction that the New World in its national life and international behavior exhibited standards superior to those of the Old. Canadians and Americans returned from Europe steeped, like Mr. Herbert Hoover, in the idea "that through three hundred years America had developed something new in a way of life of a people, which transcended all others of history," especially that "boiling social and economic caldron of Europe, with its hates and fears." Rare was the North American, addressing himself to the theme of the place of his country and his continent in the world, who did not elaborate this contrast. "As one who had the great privilege of listening only a few weeks ago to the noble and inspiring message of peace and international goodwill that the late lamented President Harding delivered to the people of Canada," one of the Canadian Prime Minister's correspondents wrote to him in 1923, "I cannot help contrasting it with the continued hypocrisy and savage utterances of European national leaders." Mackenzie King himself repeated Harding's homilies for the benefit of the gathering of imperial statesmen assembled in London later that year. He quoted, approvingly, the President's peroration, and added: "I place these words on record largely because I think they help to illustrate the new-world point of view that is in very striking contrast to the old-world attitude of the past, if not of the present, that force is always essential in the preservaion of peace." If proof of the proposition were wanted, the unregenerate statesmen of Europe were told on more than one occasion, they had only to look to North America. There, a Canadian delegate informed the Fifth Assembly of the League of Nations, people thought "in terms of peace, while Europe, an armed camp, thinks in terms of war."

There thus took hold in North America the tradition, more often asserted than analysed, that Canada and the United States dealt with the world, and especially with one another, in a manner peculiarly their own. It was not just that they had renounced war as an instrument of national policy, concluding, in the words of the *Canadian Defence Quarterly* of 1924, that "the common civilization of the two countries, the intimacy of their economic and social ties, and the impossibility of making adequate preparation for the defense of the border, all make war too remote a possibility for serious consideration." It was not even a matter of that famous unfortified frontier without fulsome reference to which no international bridge could be opened and no after-dinner speech was complete. Rather it was the conviction, stronger, if anything, on the United States side of the border than on the Canadian, that the relationship of the two countries was unlike any prevailing elsewhere in the world. Where else could be found so extended a frontier crossed so frequently and so freely with such variety of purpose by such essentially like-minded people? The uniqueness of the relationship seemed to have created an entirely new kind of international affair. The North American continent provided a prime example of what social scientists were later to call a subordinate state-system—one whose members (to quote Raymond Aron) "spontaneously live a common destiny and make a distinction between what happens within and what happens outside their geographical-historical zone." For these favored few, the ordinary rigidities of protocol and the master methods of statecraft were wholly inappropriate. "Relations between Canada and the United States," declared the *Chicago Tribune* in 1926, "are unique. To a European our relations seem naïve and unworldly. We think of Canadians as fellow North Americans. Italians do not think of Germans or Frenchmen as fellow Europeans in anything like the same sense. They are suspicious where we have confidence."

Because of that confidence (it came to be asserted) any dispute which might arise between the two countries ought to be settled bilaterally, as befitted good neighbours, without the intrusion of alien international institutions. Like the British Commonwealth, Canada and the United States developed their own version of an *inter se* doctrine according to which their quarrels should be quelled in the privacy of the family circle. Such a feeling led naturally to an array of special inter-governmental machinery, in addition to the ordinary diplomatic channels. The oldest and best known is the International Joint Commission created in 1909. It consists of a standing tribunal of six commissioners in each of its Canadian and American sections, and is authorized to deal not only with waterways disputes but in addition "any other matters of difference arising . . . along the common frontier." The Canadian principally responsible for its creation was justifiably proud of his handiwork. As he, George C. Gibbons, wrote to Sir Wilfred Laurier:

> I think you will find [it] the greatest advance ever made by way of diplomacy to settle international complications. A permanent judicial board is an experiment which, I believe, will prove a complete success. It ought to have existed long ago in Europe. The people will some day there, too, take it out of the power of any one crazy monarch to set a continent on flame.

This was the first of many subsequent occasions on which North American statesmen referred their European colleagues to the Commission as an instrument they would do well to copy if they could. "I am convinced," Mackenzie King wrote in 1923, "that it contains the new world answer to old world queries as to the most effective methods of adjusting international differences and avoiding the wars to which they give rise"; in 1942 he expressed to Franklin Roosevelt his opinion that the Commission could well serve as the basis for postwar international organization. That was expecting too much of it. But its original, and less grandiose, purpose it has served well. Mutually satisfactory solutions to all but two of the nearly forty waterways disputes referred to the Commission have been forthcoming: that it failed to produce an acceptable formula for the future of the resources of the Columbia River system (see below) is less a reflection on the institution than a warning that the best of institutions should not be overloaded.

The Canadian-American relationship resembled that of the Commonwealth relationship in another respect. Just as Lloyd George declared that Dominion status was incapable of definition, and warned of the danger of "limiting our Constitution by too many finalities," so the statesmen of North America were reluctant to give too many of their affairs the precision of formal undertakings. Their relationship, they felt, was too precious, too spiritual, almost, to be sullied by definition. Treaties were for governments whose word could not be their bond. When it was suggested to John W. Davis, formerly United States ambassador to Great Britain, that the time had come for re-negotiating the Rush-Bagot Treaty of 1817, he replied:

> A mental attitude so deeply fixed, an international habit so deeply rooted, is far more stable and lasting than any paper covenant that was ever penned. The attempt to make it a matter of formal contract is rather to degrade it than to exalt it much as if one were asked to promise in writing to observe the Ten Commandments. There it stands. Let us hold it up before our people as a thing no longer open to discussion or debate.

And this view prevailed.

Within the British Commonwealth, decades of hard commercial bargaining had convinced all but the most sentimental imperialist that the ties of empire meant little or nothing when it came down to pounds and dollars. But within North America, the special relationship of Canada and the United States was confidently expected to prevail even in the trying sphere of trade and commerce. The United States chargé d'affaires in Ottawa wrote to the Secretary of State in 1933,

> I submit that our relations with Canada are and should continue to be exceptional. . . . Our trade relations with Canada, often described as our "best customer," economically our most powerful neighbor, indissolubly an immediate part of the economic system of this hemisphere, are and must be considered on a different footing from our trade relations with distant nations or with all nations. . . .

The ideology of the Canadian-American relationship, then, consists of two propositions. First, that there exists between the two countries a community of interests and an equation of identity which render nugatory and unnecessary external mechanisms for the settlement of their disputes. Second, that insofar as they have been left alone by the twentieth century to settle their disputes, they have succeeded to a degree which other nations have not experienced and which must be their constant envy.

This ideology persists today, in the face of all evidence to the contrary. A distinguished American wrote in 1961: "No difference has arisen that has not yielded to amicable solution; no instance has arisen in which one tried to out-maneuver the other; no hard bargains have been sought and no sharp practices have fettered the sense of fairness that has prevailed. The principle of reasonableness and of friendly cooperation has been the guiding star." That same year a still more distinguished American remarked, incontrovertibly enough: "Geography has made us neighbors." But, President Kennedy (for it was he) added, "history has made us friends." History in fact made the two neighbours enemies. If they are friends today, it is in spite of history, not because of it.

Defining the Hard Issues

The selection of a list of the more important contemporary problems of the Canadian-American relationship for examination and analysis presents certain difficulties.

The national agenda are manifestly bound to differ. The more powerful of the two neighbours, with its policy problems ranging the world from Iceland to Vietnam, will not put North American affairs permanently at the top of its list. For most of the time, indeed, North American affairs will not figure on a United States priority list at all. On those infrequent occasions when they do, they figure as a different set of problems, viewed in a different perspective, from that confronting Canada. When President Kennedy went to pay his respects to Prime Minister Diefenbaker in May 1961, it was reported that a document, presumably mislaid by a member of the President's entourage, stated the agenda of Canadian-American relations from the United States' point of view in succinct language: Canada should join the Organization of American States; Canada should contribute a greater proportion of its gross national product to foreign aid; Canada should give more aid to India. In no time during the last forty years could a Canadian Prime Minister have gone to Washington with so few items on his agenda, and these all dealing with the international rather than the domestic scene. In any relationship between a powerful state and a weak state, the grievances of the latter are bound to outnumber those of the former. The Canadian-American relationship is no exception to this rule. The agenda of problems discussed in this paper inevitably resembles an agenda compiled in Ottawa more closely than an agenda compiled in Washington.

It resembles, too, an agenda prepared by intelligent laymen, rather than an agenda prepared by foreign offices. Were the discussion confined to the kinds of problems over which foreign offices, left to their own devices, execute their delicate steps of détente and démarche in the perpetual quadrille of the balance of power, the list would be shorter than it is. It would also bear scant resemblance to the problems of the real world. The problems of the real world have to do with the emotions of publics as often as with the concerns of the professional diplomatist. In democracies, diplomatists are as busy as they are because of the agitation of their publics. (Which may be why, in democracies, diplomatists and publics do not get along together very well.) A number of the items to be discussed below are problems of attitude, arising in the minds of men rather than in the actions of government, and becoming intergovernmental only because of extensive public concern on one side of the border or the other.

Finally, there is the related difficulty of dealing with issues which are essentially spurious, as distinct from issues which are real. Real issues may be defined as those which arise from some ascertainable fact: a diversion of a river, an expropriation of an industry, an incarceration of a citizen. Spurious issues may be defined as those which arise from the misapprehension of reality. It is not always easy to distinguish between the two. And issues may be no less troublesome for being spurious. Accordingly, I have included in my selection certain issues—the fear in Canada that national identity is threatened by movements of capital and culture, for example—which seem to me to be essentially spurious. There are many Canadians, some in high places, who regard them as real enough.

The "hard issues," then, as they appear below, are those which, whether they figure on a Canadian agenda or an American, whether they are of concern to publics or to foreign offices, whether they are spurious or real, seriously and protractedly harm the Canadian-American relationship. So defined, there are enough hard issues to fill a book. What follows, therefore, is not—cannot be—a checklist of inter-North American grievances, a catalog of all the complaints each country has about the other. I have selected from the score or more available those few issues which seem to me exceptionally important for the future of the relationship; or which throw new light upon its nature; or which, being unique to the relationship, illuminate the working of international society.

Defending the Continent

One problem of the Canadian-American relationship stands out first and foremost from the rest; for it, unlike the others, may be admitted to a list of "hard issues" on any of the criteria mentioned above. It is the problem of continental defense. More exactly, the problem of working out the conditions of cooperation by which the two countries, through their sovereign governments, may take part in the defence of the land-mass which is their common home. The problem figures prominently on the agenda of both; it is a preoccupation alike of publics and of public servants; it has its spurious aspects, as well as those which are rooted firmly in the realities.

Tradition and survival

The fundamental reality is the location of Canada squarely and irretrievably athwart the attack approaches of the two great nuclear antagonists, each of whom, since 1957 or earlier, has been able to devastate if not to destroy the other.

Treaties may be broken, pacts can be denounced, but geography holds its victims fast. If the United States is ever brought under atomic attack, Canada's territory, Canada's people, neutral or not, will be fearsomely scourged. The assault would come (notwithstanding Soviet submarines, Cuban missiles or satellite launchers) mainly from across the North Pole. Fallout respects no frontier. Most of what interception there might be of marauding missiles and bombers would occur over Canadian territory, and the apparatus with which it must be presumed that Soviet warheads will be armed will cause their detonation if stopped short of primary targets.

If one looks at this situation through the cool if callous eyes of an operations researcher or a systems analyst, policy becomes simplicity itself. If what is dangerous to the United States is no less dangerous to Canada, it follows that Canadians should do everything in their power to help the United States improve and perfect the means of reducing danger. They should accordingly do what they can to strengthen the apparatus of massive retaliation, and to improve the defences of the continent in case deterrence fails. But public opinion does not always or even usually respond with the logic of operations research. And a distinctive, if not the dominant, ingredient in the Canadian public's response to its unenviable positioning along the route to holocaust has been an irrational anger. Not all Canadians, not (on the evidence of pollsters) most Canadians, but certainly a great many Canadians, so far from being eager and willing to help the United States in its strategy of conflict, seem to resent the kind of uneasy existence which their proximity to the Americans has made inevitable; to resent the lack of options of which geography deprives them; and to take out that resentment not so much against the Soviet Union (where if anywhere it is properly directed) as against their friends and neighbours.

Canadian strategic intelligencers are perceptibly more sceptical than their American counterparts concerning the intentions and capabilities of the enemy. Their answers to the questions, "Would the Soviet Union attack North America if it could?" and "Could it attack if it would?" are more likely to be answered in the negative. Canadian defence authorities, both civilian and military, frankly do not think that the evidence warrants the alarmist interpretations frequently placed upon it by the American intelligence community. They know how often intelligence estimates in the United States are really weapons in that Cold War waged between the Congress and the White House, or indeed between different parts of the armed services; their confidence in the American policy machine is not fortified by the belief held by some of its members that all sorts of fiendish designs on the security of North America are concocted in the caves of Cuba. At a briefing of visitors to the headquarters of the North American Air Defense Command (NORAD), the senior American and Canadian officers present were asked whether they could detect, in their years of working together as a combined command, any significant difference in the intelligence appraisals of their respective staffs. They agreed that there was a difference, and that it consisted in the more conservative Canadian evaluation vis-à-vis the American; the United States officer in charge of the intelligence directorate remarked that in retrospect the Canadian evaluation, while more conservative, was usually more accurate.

These divergent attitudes in the apprehension of external danger naturally condition the approach to continental defence. If it is assumed that the Russians are continuously engaged in a kind of necrophiliac calculation of advantage, poised to strike at North America the moment their computers (or their instincts) tell them its annihilation may be accomplished at the cost, say, of only 17 major Soviet cities and 65 per cent of Soviet industrial capacity, the case for a merger of Canadian-American sovereignty—in the spirit of Winston Churchill's offer of Anglo-French union in the dark summer of 1940—becomes overwhelming. But if a less alarmist view is taken of Soviet intentions, there will be other countervailing considerations to take into account. The chief of these, for the Canadian government, is the effect on its capacity for independent peacekeeping of any prolonged intimacy with the cold warriors of the West.

Atomic anxieties

For all these doubts and reservations, Canada's commitments to continental defence have been by no means negligible. They include the construction, or the permitted construction, of the early warning radar networks across Canadian territory; the making available of certain flight facilities to the bombers of the Strategic Air Command; the entry (not without misgiving) into the North American Air Defense Command. But though that much was done, much more might have been done. There was no invitation to the United States to treat the territory of northern North America as a possible home for whatever bombers or missiles its defence authorities might have wanted to base there; no offer of Canadian airfields as forward bases for United States interceptor aircraft; no *carte blanche* for S.A.C. overflights (the United States command deemed it expedient to route its aerial alert force around Canada rather than over it).

That Canada was less eagerly committed than the United States to continental defence was demonstrated at the time of the Soviet-American confrontation over Cuban missile sites in October 1962. "The Government," the Secretary of State for External Affairs explained, "is trying to keep the Canadian people from getting all excited about this business." Such a response, and the general attitude of which it was a reflection, was not well received by the Pentagon.

The State Department on January 30, 1963 released to the press its famous statement declaring, "the Canadian government has not yet proposed any arrangement sufficiently practical to contribute effectively to North American defense." Prompting this unprecedentedly blunt accusation was the continuing reluctance of the Canadian government to conclude negotiations, begun in 1958 but in abeyance for the next three years, for the acquisition by Canada, under conditions of United States custody and joint control, of nuclear warheads for the four weapons systems which had been designed for them. (These were the CF-104 Starfighter squadrons in service with NATO in Western Europe; the CF-101B Voodoo jet interceptors assigned to NORAD; two squadrons of Bomarc B anti-aircraft missiles at North Bay, Ontario and La Macaza, Quebec; the Honest John ground-to-ground missiles of the Fourth Infantry Brigade Group in West Germany.) The reasons for its hesitation are complex: public opinion in Canada was deeply divided; within the Cabinet an influential minister, Howard Green, the Secretary of State for External Affairs, argued for delay on the ground that too hasty acceptance might set back the cause of disarmament; the Prime Minister was notoriously prone to indecision. The State Department's intervention acted as a catalyst of disunity within the Diefenbaker government; it fell a week later.

In the General Election campaign which followed, what to do

about nuclear weapons became the central issue. The Liberal Party, whose leader had announced its conversion to the policy of acquisition on January 12, 1963, was returned to power as a minority government. With less than half the popular vote (and that half by no means a pro-nuclear vote), Mr. Lester Pearson could hardly claim a mandate to usher Canadians over the atomic threshold. But the country, mortified by four general elections in six years, was in no mood (or so the politicians thought) to precipitate a fifth. The Liberal government was accordingly able to resume the negotiations for a nuclear weapons agreement with the United States. The agreement (the terms of which were not disclosed) was completed and went into effect before the end of the year.

It would be an error to suppose that the exchange of sandbags and conventional high explosives for nuclear warheads has removed once and for all atomic matters from the Canadian-American agenda. For Mr. Pearson's conversion to a pro-nuclear policy was for diplomatic rather than strategic reasons. Canada, he claimed, had been committed by the Diefenbaker government to a nuclear role in NATO and NORAD: "As a Canadian, I am ashamed if we accept commitments and then refuse to discharge them." It was thus to re-establish Canada's reputation as a country which could be relied upon to keep its pledged word that nuclear weapons were accepted. Having kept its word, the government would then be free to negotiate a new role, not necessarily non-nuclear but non-nuclear if necessary, as its conception of the interests of the nation and of the international community might dictate.

Procuring production

Between 1940 and 1945 the war called into being a wide variety of public enterprise: the Eldorado Mining Company, to process uranium for the atomic bomb; Polymer Corporation, for synthetic rubber; Research Enterprises, Limited, which gave Canadians their first capacity for producing precision instruments. New private firms sprang up; the capacity of established industry increased many times over. The man who presided over this industrial revolution, the late C. D. Howe, remarked at the war's end that "Never again would there be any doubt that Canada can manufacture anything that can be manufactured elsewhere."

If Canada's manufacturing capacity could not have been created without the war, neither could it have been created so dramatically without the Hyde Park Agreement. On what Franklin Roosevelt described as "a grand Sunday, April 20, 1941," he and Mackenzie

King agreed, in what was surely a unique achievement of the Canadian-American relationship, to the "general principle that in mobilizing the resources of the continent each country should provide the other with the defense articles which it is best able to produce . . . and production programs should be coordinated to this end." As far as defence production was concerned, the border was wiped out.

Having by this remarkable arrangement become a part of the continental arsenal of democracy, Canadians looked forward to more of the same when it became apparent, by 1947 or 1948, that a Cold War of indefinite duration had settled upon the world. This expectation may have been naïve, but it was intense. It was encouraged by the ideologists of Atlantic community, and by the wishful thinking of the Canadian government. Canada, more than any other NATO country, had pressed for the inclusion in the North Atlantic Treaty of Article II, which enjoins the members to "seek to eliminate conflict in their international economic policies" and to "encourage economic collaboration between any or all of them." It seemed only fair, it was indeed only logical, that nations standing together in defence of freedom (or at any rate, in defence of Western Europe), pooling their armour, their manpower, and their wits in a unique peacetime coalition force-in-being, should extend their cooperation to the production of defence matériel. And if there was any fair play, any logic, left in the world, ought not the principle of cooperative defence production be implemented in the fullest degree between the two neighbours of North America, who had cooperated so fully in time of war? What, after all, was their special relationship for?

The Korean War created an impetus for the two countries to pledge themselves to remove "as far as possible" those "barriers which impede the flow between Canada and the United States of goods essential for the common defense effort," and to "develop a coordinated programme of requirements, production and procurement." But this agreement of October 26, 1950 was agreement in principle only, for the Korean War was not total war. The centripetal forces which had drawn the members of the Grand Alliance into their wartime unity faltered in the 'fifties. After the death of Stalin (in March 1953), men of good will, good faith, and high intelligence might all the more legitimately come to quite different conclusions about the strategy and tactics of Soviet policy; lacking agreement on the nature of the challenge, how could they agree on their response? The sense of urgency which compelled the NATO nations to allocate up to half of their budgets for defence could not bring them to direct their expenditure according to the principle of comparative advantage. Moreover, in this alliance of equals, some were more equal than others. For the United States, almost every weapons system was comparatively advantageous to produce; for Iceland, almost nothing. The countries in between floundered uncertainly between the competing considerations of keeping up the strength of their defence community, and keeping up with the Joneses.

When computers and politicians disagree, the politician usually prevails; he has constituents to spur him on. So it was that "the countries in between" usually decided in favor of keeping up with the Joneses, proceeding, with only a glance at the computers, to produce as many of their own weapons systems as they could manage. Canada, which had begun its defence program by producing F-86 Sabres for the U.S.A.F. and the R.A.F., wound up by producing CF-100s for the R.C.A.F. With the end of the Korean War, a more alluring prospect came into view. A new interceptor was needed for North American defence, one which would fly faster, higher, further and to better effect than anything in service. Produced by Canadians only for Canadians, the cost of such an aircraft would have been prohibitive. But what if it were produced by Canadians for North Americans? With the United States buying the lion's share of the output, the enterprise would lie within Canadian capabilities. And what benefits to Canada would follow: jobs, know-how, kudos! The idea was irresistible. And the Liberal government of the day did not resist it.

In 1958, the new Conservative government revealed what the CF-105 program had cost the country so far. Four hundred million dollars (at least) had been expended: two aircraft had actually flown (though 35 prototypes were in varying stages of development). As much money again, perhaps much more, would be required to go into production. And there was no purchaser, other than the R.C.A.F., in sight. Giving as its primary reason the diminishing threat of attack by manned bombers, as distinct from intercontinental missiles, the government decided to scrap the whole program. The completed aircraft were sold to a junkyard for scrap. Their epitaph was pronounced by the Deputy Minister of Defence Production, in words contrasting strangely with those of C. D. Howe some fifteen years earlier: "Unfortunately, as weapons systems become increasingly complex and costly, the independent development of major military systems by Canada no longer seems possible."

The effect upon Canadians of this cancellation was traumatic. It was not just that fourteen thousand people were thrown out of work (as many as thirty thousand ultimately suffered), or even that many of the country's top technicians migrated to the greener pastures of Republic or Lockheed Aviation. It was a blow to national morale. The United States became the scapegoat. That this indictment was both irrational and unfair did not prevent its being widely accepted. Certainly the government of the day made no effort to tell Canadians what had really happened. What had really happened (as disclosed years later by the retired general who had been the government's chief military adviser at the time) was something like this. The Arrow program began as an airframe program only; into the airframe was to be fitted an American or British engine, an American weapons system (the Sparrow II), and an American communications and electronic system. In the expectation but without any guarantee that these vital components would be acceptable and available, the work on the CF-105 was put in hand. A year or two later a Canadian firm came up with what seemed like a promising engine for the Arrow, and the Canadian government, after (in General Foulkes's words) "a great deal of discussion and heart searching," decided to develop not only the airframe but the engine as well. Meanwhile the Sparrow II program was dropped by the U. S. Navy, and the Canadian government decided to take it over too. Finally, the American communication and electronic system on which the government had counted was also abandoned; when it too was taken over, the Canadian authorities found themselves having to pay for the entire cost of the aircraft. Because of miscalculation involving the numbers of reserve pilots who could be trained to handle so sophisticated a machine as the CF-105, the original requirement of 400 aircraft for the R.C.A.F. was cut back to something like 100; the unit cost soared accordingly, to $8 million. Neither the United States, nor the United Kingdom, nor any other NATO country, wanted to buy the Arrow for its own airforce. Was so devastating a series of dashed hopes bad luck, or bad management? Whichever it was, it could not properly be blamed upon the United States; but that did not stop its being blamed upon the United States.

The Arrow debacle forced upon Canadians an agonizing reappraisal of their defence production role. If, as their spokesmen had conceded, major weapons systems had become too costly for independent Canadian development, it was obviously all the more important that Canadian industries be allowed to bid for contracts in the United States on terms which would not discriminate against them just because they were Canadian, and therefore foreign. Never before was an *inter se* doctrine for defence more urgently required. The urgency was recognized in Washington, and the doctrine duly emerged, early in 1960, in the form of the Defence Production Sharing Program.

This Program, described as "a Cold War version of the 1941 Hyde Park Agreement," has led to the waiver, in Canada's favour, of the "Buy American" legislation which would have imposed a handicap of from 6 to 12 per cent on Canadian bids for contracts in competition with United States industry; it has exempted certain defence items from duty; it has produced security clearances which would not otherwise have been forthcoming. For its part, the Canadian government has in various ways subsidized Canadian firms so as to allow them to bid competitively with their United States rivals enjoying comparable concessions from the American government. Since the Program went into effect in 1959, more than 300 Canadian firms have done more than $605 millions of defence business in the United States, much of which they would not have gained without it.

Raw materials and defence

Rational use of raw materials for the common defence has been harder to come by in North America than rational use of weapons manufacturing facilities. Consider petroleum. Oil (when refined) has much the same properties and delivers much the same performance whatever its country of origin; it has an alternative market in the "peaceful" sector of the economy; its successful development creates an economic complex which can sustain the development and well-being of regions, even of nations. None of these things may be said, or said with so little qualification, of manufactured weapons. There thus spring to the defence of important raw materials industries puissant lobbyists—lobbyists for whose activities the governmental system of the United States seemed at times to have been almost expressly designed.

In 1958, yielding finally to the ceaseless pressure of domestic oil producers, the United States administration placed Canadian oil imports under that quota system previously confined to imports from the Middle East. This move was justified as being essential to national defence; the United States could not afford to become dependent upon sources of supply outside its territory and so likely to be cut off in times of tension or international conflict. While it was clear enough (as the Suez crisis had demonstrated) that oil from Kuwait or Iraq could not always be counted upon, it was by no means clear who (other than their competitors) would blow up the international pipelines of North America. "Oil in Alberta," Mr. Pearson remarked in January 1958, "is as safe from hostile interference, and as available for United States use, as is oil in Oklahoma." The banning of Canadian imports on grounds of national security was, of course, the feeblest of fictions. "What is really being defended by the artificial Federal restriction," the *Wall Street Journal* pointed out, "is the competitive position of the marginal United States oil producer."

This form of disguised protection was all the harder to take in Canada in view of the fact that, to a considerable degree, the capacity of the Canadian oil industry had been expanded at the urging of the United States government which, during the Korean War, was anxious to extend the petroleum reserves of North America. It accordingly drew from Ottawa some of the most strongly worded diplomatic protests that have ever passed between the two capitals. "The Canadian government cannot accept the view," a note from Ottawa to Washington declared early in January 1958, "that there is any justification for United States limitations on oil coming from Canada." In response to pressure from the Canadian government (and, it may be, in response to pressure from United States international oil interests), the Administration periodically relaxed the restrictions it periodically imposed. But the threat of restriction remains, and will remain as long as Canada is not clearly and specifically exempted from the national security provisions of United States raw materials policy. On any dispassionate strategic analysis, it ought to be exempted. But that is not to say it will be.

Uranium, unlike petroleum, has been used mainly for military purposes ever since the summer of 1942 when ore was shipped from the deposits at Great Bear Lake, near the Arctic Circle, for the development of the atomic bomb. The failure after the end of World War II to achieve international control over atomic energy was followed by the American government's decision to accumulate what Ralph Lapp rightly calls "the incredible stockpile" of nuclear weapons. (By 1967, it has been estimated, this stockpile will consist of more than 1,000 tons of fissionable materials, the equivalent of 200,000 Hiroshima-type bombs.) This in turn stimulated exploration, development, and exploitation of further sources of uranium in Canada. The search was fantastically successful. The Gunnar discovery in Saskatchewan of the early 1950's was followed soon afterwards by the disclosure of the huge low-grade deposits in the Blind River-Algoma region of Northern Ontario. The value of Canadian uranium sold to the United States Atomic Energy Commission in 1958 was $262,700,000, more than the value of nickel (previously the most important mineral export) sold abroad that year. The speculative fervor which earlier in the 1950's had drawn hundreds of gamblers into the board rooms of Toronto brokers now seemed to grip the government itself. The Province of Ontario invested $10 million (private investors put up $45 million) to build a model town in the wilderness.

> There are few places in the world more beautiful than Algoma in the Canadian autumn, when the trees are red, brown and gold. The waters of a thousand little lakes glisten and the rocky hills are massive and magnificent. These rocks have now come to life. . . . The resulting activity is converting an area which had been the reserve of the hunter and fisherman into a furiously growing industrial complex centered in a thriving well-planned community, Elliott Lake. . . .

These words, which sound as if they might have been written by the promoter of a Florida swamp lot or an acre of Arizona desert, were actually written by Lester Pearson, in whose constituency of Algoma-Blind River the great uranium find was located.

The boom was short-lived. Even as early as 1957 it was apparent that world production of uranium was far outstripping demand. The United States, which bought 90 per cent of all Canadian sales abroad, was fast developing its own uranium mining industry on the Colorado Plateau. In November 1959 the United States Atomic Energy Commission announced that it would not exercise any of its options to buy Canadian uranium after 1962-63; existing contracts which were to have expired in that year would be stretched over a further three-year period. The sequel was cruel for the hewers of pitchblende in Blind River. Elliott Lake, which had attained a population of 25,000 by 1959, lost 10,000 of its inhabitants by the end of 1960; the mining force itself declined from 10,500 to 2,900. As at the time of the Arrow's cancellation, the United States again served as a scapegoat. Thus the verdict of a Canadian economist reached in the detachment of his study: "The United States exported to Canada the adverse effects of over-supply, thereby protecting its own uranium industry and satisfying the demands of the mining 'lobby' in Washington." The verdict of the embattled citizenry of Elliott Lake, left in the lurch amid their worthless housing and their foetid water supply, may best be left to the imagination.

Both verdicts blamed Washington. With what justice? It is true that the Agreement for Cooperation on Civil Uses of Atomic Energy, signed by Canada and the United States on June 15, 1955, referred in Article VI to the development of Canadian uranium production "under arrangements and contracts now in effect," adding that "these arrangements shall remain in full force and effect except as modified or revised by mutual agreement." It is true that in the event the arrangements were modified unilaterally and that, as an American authority has observed, "Canadian uranium producers were assured of a market in the United States only until American producers required that same market." But this hardly sustains a charge of bad faith. The principle *pacta sunt servanda* governing international dealings must always be understood to be accompanied by the principle *clausula rebus sic stantibus:* governments abide by their undertakings, provided that circumstances do not drastically change. The circumstances of the uranium industry did drastically change, and not without warning. The blame for the disaster which has overtaken the Canadian uranium mining industry may be more properly placed at the door of those governments which, entrusted with its care, allowed their optimism to run away with their judgment.

Trading Without Tears

Commerce and the continent

Canada has always been, is now, and probably always will be, a trading nation. Canada has always had, has now, and probably always will have, a staple economy. Recent development in the lee of sheltering tariffs of some secondary industry is of less significance than the addition of new staples to the traditional staffs of economic life, nickel, oil, uranium, joining fish, furs, wheat and wood. Canada has for the last thirty years been largely dependent on the American market for selling what she has to sell, and hence for its prosperity. In 1933 R. B. Bennett declared he could do more for Canada if he could set American tariff rates than as Prime Minister: such a remark from a Canadian Prime Minister in 1963 might exaggerate the degree of dependence, but not much. Canada has usually sold over 40 per cent of all her exports (with the important exceptions of farm and fish products) to the United States since the turn of the century; since 1957, over 60 per cent. In the case of forest products (of which newsprint is the most valuable), the figure typically has been higher than 75 per cent; in the case of uranium (as we have seen), as high as 90 per cent. There has been, and remains, as Professor Jacob Viner has observed, "a close and favorable correlation between Canadian prosperity and the American level of consumption of Canadian products."

Across the border, the pattern of trade changes dramatically. The commitment of every Administration since Franklin Roosevelt took office to the precepts of freer trade must not obscure the essential fact that the American economy is a comparatively closed economy. With its great size, its high level of productivity, its wealth and diversity of natural resources, it could hardly be otherwise. In trade, as in so much else, Canada is less important to the United States than is the United States to Canada. This is not to say that it is marginal. One fifth of United States exports are bought by Canada. Allowing for the fact that foreign trade is itself a less important sector of the American than of the Canadian economy, it remains true, as one study has pointed out, that "Canada's trade with the United States is sufficiently large that a significant number of individual producers and buyers in the United States rely quite heavily upon trans-border trade."

The two fundamental facts of North American geography—the proximity of its two countries, and the larger market and productivity of one of them—have between them created a trade pattern of exceptional imbalance. But on the face of it, this should cause no great problem. Unlike many trading partners, Canada and the United States have economies which nicely complement each other. In return for raw materials and semi-processed commodities, exported to the United States, Canada may buy—does buy in great quantity—manufactured goods and such non-Canadian delicacies as Florida oranges (and Florida vacations). When the scales tipped too far in the Americans' favor, Canadians could do without their power lawn-mowers, their orange juice, and their winter sojourns at Miami Beach. This simple prescription, for all its appeal to the chartered accountant and the sterner sort of moralist, is unrealistic. It neglects the crucial factors of aspiration, proximity, and availability. Canada may be a staple-exporting nation, but Canadians are not simple peasants. Most of them live in large cities, and hanker after the material benefits of this life as much as any North Americans. Those cities, moreover, are cheek by jowl with the United States. Living so close to their neighbours, Canadians are made instantly aware of discrepancies in standards of living; when they are not crossing the border for bargains, television and magazines bring strident reminders of American affluence into their homes. They know only too well that the cost of being Canadian—in the most literal sense—is higher than the cost of being American. How much higher they are prepared to put up with must be the constant preoccupation of every Canadian government; too high a cost will cause many to exchange their Canadian for American citizenship. If emigration is not to become a rout, there are limits to the amount of austerity that may safely be prescribed.

Capital: the highest stage of imperialism?

The over-all commercial policy of a Canadian government may follow one or other of two very different courses. It may tolerate and even encourage the natural pattern of trans-border trade wherein Canadians buy so much more from the United States than Americans buy from Canada, allowing the imbalance to be corrected by capital inflows from American investors. Or it may discourage and even interfere with the movements of goods and capital from the United States into the Dominion, hoping that various protectionist devices to stimulate the growth of manufacturing capacity at home will eventually cause the gap in living standards to close, resorting meanwhile to appeals to patriotism.

From 1948 to 1957, the Liberal government led by Mr. L. S. St. Laurent (and, in the economic field, by the redoubtable C. D. Howe), was content to follow the first of these courses. The gap in the standards of living narrowed, but the payments gap widened alarmingly. Financial crises were avoided by the stream of capital which poured into the Dominion from American investors avid to avoid the harassments and uncertainties which were becoming the lot of nonresident owners in other parts of the world. By 1957 the Canadian-American relationship exhibited yet another feature unique in the affairs of nations: a degree of ownership by citizens of one country of the resources and industries of the other that was to be found nowhere else in the world. "The heavy influx of American investment," John Diefenbaker told his audience at Dartmouth College in his first speech as Prime Minister delivered in the United States, "has resulted in some 60 per cent of our main manufacturing industries, and a larger proportion of our mine and oil production, being owned and controlled by United States interests. . . . There is," he added, "an intangible sense of disquiet in Canada over the political implications of large-scale and continuing external ownership and control of Canadian industries."

The Prime Minister owed more than he admitted on that occasion to this "intangible sense of disquiet"; skillfully exploited by himself and his Conservative colleagues, it had been as much as anything responsible for the unpredicted end of Liberal rule. "If the Liberal government is re-elected," Mr. Diefenbaker declared early in 1957, "Canada will become a virtual forty-ninth state in the American Union." The Liberal government was not re-elected; fear that had the Liberals been returned to power they would have been less than properly concerned to protect the country's resources from the "depredations of Texas buccaneers" played a large part in their defeat.

During the six years of Mr. Diefenbaker's regime, the climate for foreign investment, though not overtly hostile, was not particularly salubrious. Most interested Americans expressed unconcealed pleasure at the prospect of a Pearson government and a return, so they believed, to the easy-going days of the St. Laurent-Howe era. Their pleasure did not last as long as Mr. Pearson's so-called "sixty days of decision." Before the end of the first two months of Liberal government, the Minister of Finance brought down a budget which discriminated with unprecedented severity against United States investment in Canada.

A shrewd and knowledgeable official at the Canadian desk of the State Department would have been dismayed at this development, but he need not have been surprised. He would have known enough about the Canadian political scene to understand how much of a handicap Mr. Pearson's previous association with "the old Liberal gang" had hurt his political prospects, and how important it was that the new Prime Minister showed himself to be his own man. He would have known about Mr. Pearson's methods of delegation, and of his close friendship with Mr. Walter Gordon, and would have guessed accordingly that the Minister of Finance would have been allowed the freest possible hand in the shaping of his first budget. He would have known enough about businessmen who forsake business for politics to bet that Mr. Gordon would bite the hand that fed him. He would have read the Report of the Royal Commission on Canada's Economic Prospects (the Gordon Report), and Mr. Gordon's little book, *Troubled Canada* (1961), which even more clearly set out the standard remedy for economic ills of the chartered accountant—tighten your belt and live within your means. He would therefore have been amply prepared for Mr. Gordon's budget centre-pieces: one, a measure allowing tax benefits to Canadian companies increasing their component of Canadian ownership; another, effective on budget night, a tax of 30 per cent on sales by Canadians of shares of Canadian companies to foreigners in excess of $50,000.

Nothing (it has been said) is more timid than a million dollars —unless it is a billion dollars. Capital was never more craven than the day after Mr. Gordon's night before. The skies of Canada were dark with flights of foreign funds. The clumsy retraction of the 30 per cent tax measure soon afterwards did not signify any basic change in policy, only a belated recognition that the device in question would not work. Close on the heels of the budget came the proposals of the Kennedy Administration for improving the American international balance of payments position—proposals which threatened to dry up the stream of American investment in Canada more effectively than any Canadian finance minister had dreamed of, much less desired. Whether Mr. Kennedy and his officials at the United States Treasury were ill-informed of the extent to which their proposals would adversely affect the Canadian economy, or whether they intended to retaliate for the inhospitality of the budget, remains a matter for conjecture.

Towards investment from abroad in their economies, nations may exhibit one or other of two attitudes. They either welcome it with open arms and open markets, or discourage it by fear and suspicion. Foreign capital may be seen as a means to national fulfilment, or it may appear as a threat to national identity. The first is the characteristic attitude of relatively mature societies in which the makers of public policy, and the public itself, know enough about economic life to appreciate two of its basic facts: that there can be no development without capital from somewhere, and that capital from almost anywhere is scarce. The second is the characteristic attitude of societies recently cut loose from colonial rule whose leaders are schooled in the belief that foreign capital has been the instrument of their past captivity and threatens their future freedom. Accepting uncritically the Leninist line that there is a surplus of capital among the developed nations of the world, believing the entrepreneur to be willy-nilly an enslaver of the colonial proletariat, they treat any investor interesting himself in their affairs with all the warmth and generosity accorded a tarantula in the bananas.

Of these two attitudes, Canadian spokesmen over the past few years have exhibited the second more often that the first. "I believe that Canadians should declare their economic independence of the United States. I believe that political and economic independence go hand in hand." These words, spoken by the Leader of the Opposition in 1956, are closely paraphrased in the speeches of almost every important Canadian politician of the last decade.

In addition to relying on thread-bare doctrines of economic determinism, the case for lessening the degree of Canada's dependence upon United States capital is supported by a detailed bill of particulars against foreign corporate behavior. Firms located in Canada but owned by Americans are said to have a harmful effect upon Canadian life. They are charged with keeping their common stock from prospective Canadian investors; excluding Canadians from high managerial positions; withholding information from Canadian governments; failing, at the instigation of their head offices, to compete in the American market; buying American, instead of Canadian; providing little benefit to the host economy in the way of research; being laggards and sluggards in contributing towards Canadian charities and philanthropies. It is a damning indictment—if true.

This is not the place to conduct either prosecution or defence of the policies and practices of United States subsidiaries in Canada. But a few general observations may be useful. The first is that the truth of the indictment has not yet been established, despite considerable investigation. Lacking proof of guilt, it is customary to presume innocence. The Canadian government, having (so it believes) a vested interest in finding fault with foreign corporate behavior, has taken refuge in the assertion that the kind of activity to which it objects is difficult and even impossible to prove. There are few, if any, reputable political economists on either side of the border who would accept that contention.

A second point concerns prospective remedies. To the extent that practices harmful to the Canadian nation are proven to exist, they are not likely to be abolished by juggling personnel. Corporate malefactions, Canadian or American-controlled, can only be dealt with by public policy. Parliament, as Harry Johnson properly observes, "and not a group of Canadian stockholders foisted on the foreign companies by fiscal discrimination or political blackmail, is the appropriate guardian of the public interest."

A third observation relates to causes. If the problem of United States-controlled investment in Canada is real, rather than spurious, it is (again quoting Professor Johnson)

> largely one that Canada has created for itself by its policy of protection of manufacturing: the tariff creates a profit incentive to foreign firms to establish branch plants and subsidiaries in Canada, in order to produce in Canada inside the tariff wall instead of exporting to Canada over the

tariff wall, and it is consistent to say the least to defend protection yet complain of its effect in stimulating foreign investment in the country.

Finally, responsibility. In his 1963 budget address, the Canadian Minister of Finance warned that by acquiescing in the trend to American ownership, his countrymen were "sacrificing our birthright, the birthright which our forefathers laboured so hard to hand on to us." That way of putting it does a certain violence to history: a governor-general of Canada, used to the hustle and drive of his Victorian England, noted long ago that "Canadians are undoubtedly . . . devoid of energy—they do not go ahead as people do in the States—in fact Canada is being developed by American and British money and there is comparatively little money in Canadian national undertakings." So much for the labor of our forefathers. Their descendants have followed their example. The innate caution of the Canadian investing temperament persists as strongly sixty years on. If American investors now own so much of Canada's oil and gas, pulp and paper, minerals and manufacturing, it is because Canadians have preferred to put their capital into government bonds and life insurance. (Canadian insurance companies are by law restricted from investing more than 15 per cent of their assets in common stock; their practice is to invest barely 5 per cent.) Canadians can start buying back their birthright—most of it—whenever they want to pay for it.

Protection and prosperity

Both Canada and the United States have adhered to the ideology of freer trade, with the world outside and with each other. Both have allowed their doctrinal commitment to be marred by protectionist practices. Protection by one country becomes a problem for the other. The magnitude of the problem is greater for Canada, the welfare of Canadians being more dependent upon access to the American market than the welfare of Americans upon access to the Canadian market. But it is no small problem for the United States either.

Canadian protectionism has a stronger ideological justification than does American protectionism. To bring and hold together a nation of quarreling provinces and rival regions, to prevent these from individually or collectively throwing in their lot with the great neighbour to the south, powerful controls at the center have always been required. Because the state is the defender of Canadian unity, there is such a wide range of governmental activity in a society not naturally given to *dirigiste* solutions. Government marketing of wheat, government operation of transportation, above all government control of communications.

All this is known as the National Policy. The one politician who seemed to depart from it too drastically by advocating reciprocity—free trade between Canada and the United States—was defeated in a General Election largely on the strength of the sentiment "No truck nor trade with the Yankees." Fifty years after Laurier's downfall, Canadian politicians still shy away from the logic of continental commercial union.

The throttle of the National Policy (some critics might say the choke) has been the tariff. In the sunlight of protection, secondary industry in Canada has taken root and sprouted. No nation thinks itself complete without it. None wants to be hewer of wood or drawer of water for neighbours. This has nothing, or very little, to do with economics. The approach of Canadian governments may be described in the famous words of Professor Hallstein: "We are not in business, we are in politics." But whereas the promoters of the Economic Community sought to use the tariff as an instrument of European unity, Canadian Prime Ministers, from Macdonald to Pearson, have sought to use it as an instrument of North American separatism.

Joined to so fundamental a purpose so implacably pursued, the Canadian tariff against United States goods is not likely to be abolished, whatever the economic arguments in favor of abolition. Since the issue is political, it is best discussed in political terms. Does the Canadian tariff, to the extent that it protects domestic industry from foreign competition, really contribute to the development of a strong Canadian nation? Politicians and their court-economists have argued, or more often assumed, that it does. More independent analysis suggests that it does not. "A Tokugawa policy," as the economist H. C. Eastman has described the chauvinistic manifestations of Canadian commercial policy:

> is inadequate for furthering Canada's traditional ambitions of achieving high income and international influence. This policy lowers the Canadian standard of living by diverting production away from those things Canadians can produce best. It also lowers Canadian influence [in the world] because the source of Canadian power, more than that of many countries, is based on information and persuasion and this is only accepted from those who participate in the affairs at issue and who meet their own problems successfully.

Harry Johnson has written:

> If the public is to be taxed for the privilege of having a national identity—which is what the protectionists are really arguing for—there are far more worthy monuments to national independence than a second-rate manufacturing sector that could be constructed with the money—a decent social security system, a comprehensive public health programme, beautiful cities free of slums, a truly free and high quality educational system, a truly bilingual culture.

It would be idle to pretend that the mood of the moment in Ottawa is receptive to advice of this kind. On the ashes of the 1963 budget discriminating against American capital has risen the phoenix of protection discriminating against American imports. In October 1963 the Pearson government announced its determination to lessen the dependence of the Canadian automobile industry on parts imported from the United States (valued, in 1962, at roughly $400 million). The ingenious proposal by which it is intended that this be accomplished (it involves giving automobile firms that increase their export of parts an exemption of duty on imports of automobiles and parts to an amount equal to the value of their export increases) may not be protectionist according to any of the provisions of the General Agreement on Tariffs and Trade, but it is frankly protectionist in spirit, and was bitterly opposed by the Kennedy Administration. "It may be hard to make a case [against the Canadian plan] under international trade rules," an American official conceded, "but there are lots of United States-Canada negotiations coming up and we'll remember this."

The barriers of bureaucracy

Covert protectionism assumes many forms. They include the content protection of the Canadian government's plan for the automotive industry. They include the various escape hatches used by both Canada and the United States to protect particular industries and special interests from severe or unexpected injury resulting from lower tariffs and higher quotas. They include the national security provisions of United States trade legislation (discussed above). They include anti-dumping measures imposed by administrative authority. They include as well the practices of arbitrary valuation and classification of goods coming in under existing tariff schedules.

It was an American authority who wrote, forty years ago, that if he could write the Administrative Act, he cared not who wrote the rates of duty. Since then exporters on both sides of the border have had reason to regret the barriers placed by bureaucrats in the path of trade. Wearisome and unnecessary delays in clearance, complicated procedures, arbitrary decisions, whimsical and bizarre classifications reminiscent of the celebrated *Punch* cartoon—"Cats is 'dogs' and rabbits is 'dogs' and so's parrots, but this 'ere 'Tortis' is a insect"—may protect domestic producers as effectively as any tariff wall or quota restriction. They have been aptly called the "invisible barriers to trade": as befits the invisible, they present, as the authors of one study acknowledge, "vast complexity and subtle and obscure depths." If it is sometimes hard to ascertain their impact, it is all the more difficult to determine their intent. As long as they are solely the product of carelessness and lassitude, mutual reform is self-evidently necessary and not too troublesome to bring about. But if they exist with the knowledge and indeed at the instigation of the national policy makers as a substitute for other forms of protection, their discovery will lead to ill-feeling and their eradication will tax the most patient diplomacy—so the two North American neighbours have long been aware.

Sharing Resources

Resources of nature

Natural frontiers exist between nations, but the border between Canada and the United States is not one of them. Birds fly over it, fish swim through it, ore bodies lie under it, stands of timber straddle it, rivers traverse it. As in the movement of trade, so in the disposition of resources. The continent is an economic unit. Its bisection is political, not geographic. What nature joined together, Canadians have sought to sunder.

Thoughtful people on both sides of the border have denounced the sundering of North America as wasteful, inefficient, and unnecessary. Why not, they argue, develop the continent as nature intended it to be developed, exploiting the resources of each country for the enrichment of both? Why should (to take a favorite example), the Dominion government subsidize uneconomic coal from Nova Scotia or Alberta when all the anthracite it needs lies just across Lake Ontario? Two thoughtful people at Hyannis Port, Massachusetts, reaffirmed in May 1963 "the desire of the two governments to cooperate in a rational use of the continent's resources: oil, gas, electricity, strategic metals and minerals"; as one was the Prime

Minister of Canada and the other the President of the United States, their reaffirmation had more than routine significance. But it is always easier to reaffirm general principles than to put policies into effect. The rationalization of the natural resources of North America runs into two powerful obstacles: the fear, strong in the junior partner, that economic integration may imperil national identity; the pressure, strong in both partners, from private interests wanting to protect themselves from foreign competition.

Of all the resources of nature, two in particular have been the cause of difficulty between Canada and the United States. Disputes over fisheries make up a considerable part of the diplomatic history of North America. In recent years the two countries have been engaged in a protracted argument over the legal limits of territorial waters. The United States, as a maritime power with far-flung global interests, has clung to its time-honored doctrine of the three-mile limit. Canada, with its coastal fisheries to protect from foreign encroachment, has held out for twelve miles. A compromise solution, put forward by Canada at two international conferences on the Law of the Sea, failed to gain acceptance. Ottawa thereupon resorted to unilateral action. In November 1962, it proclaimed Canadian sovereignty over the waters of the Bay of Fundy (48 miles wide at the mouth). As the alleged trespassers were Soviet trawlers, suspected of having less interest in the Maritime fisheries than in the radar defences of North America, the United States was disposed to accept this *fait accompli* without demur. In June 1963, the Canadian government announced that it had decided "to establish a 12-mile exclusive fisheries zone along the whole of Canada's coastline, as of mid-May 1964, and to implement the straight baseline system at the same time as the basis from which Canada's territorial sea and exclusive fishing zone shall be measured." Its objective this time was clearly to exclude American fishermen, not Soviet trawlers, and the Leader of the Opposition warned that unilateral action, taken by a small power against the wishes of a greater, was not always effective and could lead to retaliation and trouble. Mr. Diefenbaker may yet be proved correct in his warning: but it does not at this moment seem likely that there will develop between Canada and the United States a "fish war" of the kind which has marred the relations of two other NATO allies greatly discrepant in power—Iceland and the United Kingdom—with its tragi-comic overtones of gunboat diplomacy and minatory White Papers.

Falling water is to twentieth-century North American diplomacy what fisheries were to the nineteenth century's. Hydroelectricity is not just an ordinary resource of nature. It provides communities with the means of existence; and if withdrawn may cause the death of those communities. This being the case, international sales of hydroelectric power could safely take place only under conditions of perfect confidence and trust, in the expectation of assured sources of supply and renewal of contracts in perpetuity. Even when, as between Canada and the United States, such conditions were satisfied more fully than as between most other neighbouring countries, there was always a risk in the sale of power. The future being inscrutable, the rate of economic growth notoriously difficult to predict, it was always to be borne in mind that a government which, in all good faith, had sanctioned the export of surplus power to the other country, would discover in ten or twenty years' time that it needed it for its own development. How then repatriate it without an act of war?

Early awareness of these considerations led the Canadian government in 1907 to introduce legislation prohibiting contracts providing for the export of electric power from exceeding one year's duration. This was a case of closing the barn door after the mare escaped, for during the years immediately prior to the act in question certain private Canadian power companies had entered into export commitments to United States industry for periods as long as 85 years. They thus took on, in the words of the Minister of Trade and Commerce recalling their deed half a century later, "the responsibility of a public utility to maintain continuity of supply for [United States] customers." The Act of 1907 remained in force until 1959, when it was superseded by the National Energy Board Act. This legislation likewise sought to prevent unwise alienation of power resources, though on terms yielding somewhat to the concept of continental rationalization: all proposed power exports had to be licensed by the government's energy board; no contracts could exceed 25 years; the Board was required to certify that any power exported did not exceed the surplus remaining after due allowance had been made for "the reasonably foreseeable requirements for use in Canada"; the Board was to satisfy itself that the price of any power sold to the United States was "just and reasonable in relation to the public interest" in Canada.

In October 1963, the Minister of Trade and Commerce announced the features of what he called "a national power policy" in which national interest and the kind of continental approach endorsed by the two gentlemen at Hyannis Port were to be reasonably balanced. It was apparent from his announcement that the

Canadian Government now viewed less apprehensively than in former years the consequences of selling power to the Americans. For this change of mind, technology was more responsible than politics. "The nature of the power industry today," the Minister stated, "is very different from what it was in 1907 and in most of the intervening years." Electricity might now be carried without serious loss over long distance transmission lines, and through a national and even international continental grid power shifted from where it was plentiful to where it was scarce. Thus, "it would be in the national interest, in suitable cases, to licence the export of large scale remote hydro or other power projects which would not be viable unless supported by the export for long periods of a significant portion of the power generated." The electricity of Labrador might now be sold in New York City.

The electricity of British Columbia might, by the same policy, be sold in the United States Pacific Northwest, though under what terms was in January 1964 not wholly clear. The future of the immense hydroelectric power potential of the Columbia River basin had been the subject of negotiation between Canada and the United States for fifteen years after the end of World War II. What had to be decided was not whether power would be exported, and at what price and for how long, but how it would be generated, in what location and by what country. Looking to the future, as did General A. G. L. McNaughton, the chief Canadian negotiator, one could see a Canada which would require all the power the Columbia system offered, and more; he accordingly devised a breath-taking scheme for the diversion of the river within Canadian territory, ensuring, as he thought, Canadian control of this most precious resource for all time. Looking to the present, as did the American negotiators (and the Premier of British Columbia), one could see a power-hungry complex in the adjoining states of Washington, Oregon and Northern California, needing the electricity here and now and ready to pay for it if an acceptable deal could be worked out. The ensuing dispute, too complex to be dealt with here, defied the efforts of negotiators for nearly a decade. Finally, a treaty was signed on January 17, 1961. It was thought by its principal signatories, President Eisenhower and Prime Minister Diefenbaker, to have laid down guidelines and principles for international development of the Columbia which would provide both countries with a fair share of its benefits, and to have struck a reasonable compromise between the long term and the short.

General McNaughton thought otherwise. Cast to one side by

the government, he undertook in what was almost a one-man crusade to persuade the people of Canada that the proposed Treaty (which had been ratified by the United States Senate but not yet approved by Parliament) was a sell-out, the result of greed and of ignorance. "We did not," he declared, "have the topographical maps of the rivers in our own country; we did not even know the elevations and critical points along the river, or the volume of flow." Along the Columbia, knowledge meant power, in every sense of the word.

These grave criticisms—the more impressive for the unquestioned integrity and expertise of the critic—had the effect of causing the incoming Liberal administration to enter, in 1963, into new negotiations on the Columbia treaty. It did not, to be sure, open up the bulky Columbia dockets once again. But it did reach a new agreement, embodied in a protocol to the 1961 treaty, which gave the Canadian and British Columbia governments better financial terms than the original. The protocol was signed at Washington by President Johnson and Prime Minister Pearson on January 22, 1964. Only future generations will be in a position to know whether this crucial decision of the Canadian government was far-sighted statesmanship or spineless surrender.

Resources of labor

If the central governments of North America have on occasion thrown up barriers to trade and hoarded their natural resources, they have been generous to each other's labor forces. The border of their countries, notwithstanding its army of immigration and customs officials, may be crossed by a Canadian or a United States citizen (if he is not of Asian origin) as easily as he may cross any in the world. Every year, millions of North Americans take advantage of the ease of entry into their neighbour's nation. Most are tourists; many are on business; a surprising number live in one country and work in the other; even more are citizens of one country and live and work in the other. Numerous conventions—not least important one dealing with income tax—facilitate this common market for North American employment.

The market offers greater advantages to Canadians than to Americans, for it expands their opportunities tenfold. But it is less advantageous to Canada, for it deprives the Dominion of the skills and services of the kind of Canadians it needs most. Three-and-three-quarter million Americans of Canadian origin now live in the United States; they are the third largest and possibly the most intelligent group of immigrants in that country. (They include one of the three American contributors to the present volume.) This emigration of talent goes on apace and shows little sign of slowing down. "You have become," an American audience has been told by one who stayed behind, "such a mecca for scientists, musicians, or invertebrate palaeontologists that you threaten to leave the rest of us permanently as refugees for the second class."

The loss of so much of its elite to the United States is not, for Canada, a hard issue. But it is a hard fact. Canadians will have to put up with it as best they can until that day when the standards of life and opportunity in the Dominion become commensurate with those in the Republic. That day is distant still.

Occasionally the free and easy movement of North Americans across the border has been impeded by government. During the early years of World War II, the United States imposed regulations requiring that Canadians wishing to visit the country for whatever reason would have to equip themselves with passports and visas. Another lapse occurred ten years later, at the height and as a consequence of the McCarthy hysteria. Visiting Canadians suspected of association with "subversive" elements were sometimes subjected to insistent and often ignorant interrogation at the border about their political beliefs and affiliations; two or three distinguished scholars suffered hardship by this practice; wholly innocent people found their names on mysterious lists prepared by the Federal Bureau of Investigation and themselves barred, in some cases permanently barred, from entering the United States. A wave of hostility swept through the Canadian intellectual community at these un-American activities, instilling prejudices against the United States which to this day have not been wholly overcome. Fortunately the mania subsided before further damage was done, and more liberal and civilized authority resumed its friendly watch along the border.

Of roughly 1,500,000 trade union members in Canada, about 75 per cent belong to labor organizations having American affiliates and head offices in the United States. The five largest Canadian unions, with a total membership in excess of 300,000, all have an "international" connection. "There is nothing like this," a Canadian trade union official has pointed out, "anywhere else in the world, and it has been a perennial subject of uneasiness, real or feigned, among Canadian employers, some groups of Canadian workers, and considerable sections of the general public." To the extent that this uneasiness reflects a concern for the national interest, rather than a desire to weaken the trade union movement, it represents a fear lest the sovereignty of Canada be placed in jeopardy by the domination of Canadian by American organized labor, and apprehension that the best interests of both the Canadian nation and its labor force may be sacrificed by foreign trade union officials sensitive only to the needs of their domestic rank and file and of their own government.

The most influential Canadian labor organization, the Canadian Labour Congress (CLC), has done its best to reassure Canadians that its association with the AFL-CIO has been beneficial not only to itself but to Canada. Canadian labor, so its spokesmen have claimed, derived benefits but no disadvantages from its fraternal association with American labor. Above all, Canadian unions were wholly autonomous: they made their own decisions and shaped their own policies as they saw fit.

Until recent years there seemed no good reason to doubt these assurances. But during the 1950's a dark shadow fell upon international trade unionism in North America. Into a number of Canadian labor disputes there was intruded the power and authority, often in an ugly and violent form, of the American affiliate. The gravest of these intrusions was into a jurisdictional dispute on the Great Lakes. Unruly and unlawful activity by the Seafarers' International Union (SIU), the major union of Great Lakes seamen, led its Canadian affiliate, the CLC, to expel it and to charter a new union, the Canadian Maritime Union (CMU) in its place. Despite its expulsion from the CLC, the SIU remained an affiliated member in good standing of the AFL-CIO. Between the SIU and the CMU there broke out a bitter struggle; the nastier tactics of waterfront warfare were frequently resorted to. The American SIU boycotted Canadian ships in American ports; a Canadian union retaliated by striking the locks, thereby bringing shipping on the Great Lakes to a standstill. In 1962 the Canadian Government created a Royal Commission to investigate. Its report, published a year later, condemned the tactics of the SIU in the strongest possible language; it described its leader, Harold C. Banks, as being made "of the stuff of the Capones and the Hoffas of whom the dictators throughout history, from the earliest times to the totalitarians, Hitler and Stalin, are prototypes . . . a bully, cruel, dishonest, greedy, powerhungry, contemptuous of the law." A government-imposed trusteeship, to supervise the activities of all locals of unionized Canadian seamen, was urgently recommended.

To this juncture the dispute had been an essentially Canadian affair though, as the Prime Minister admitted, it had international implications. (One of these was that Hal Banks had been an American import.) The CLC and other Canadian unions strongly supported the proposal to bring the seamen's unions under government trusteeship. Their American affiliates were just as strongly opposed. "The SIU," declared the President of the AFL-CIO, Mr. George Meany, "deserves the support of all AFL-CIO affiliates in its fight against the destruction of free trade unionism in the Canadian maritime industry." The United States Secretary of Labor, Mr. Willard Wirtz, stated that private, not government, trusteeship was the answer, and allowed himself to be understood as having claimed that there would have been a private trusteeship but for the obduracy of the CLC in refusing to allow an American majority. These interventions were not well received in Canada. The Prime Minister described Mr. Meany's statement as "shocking," and Mr. Wirtz's statement as "unhelpful." The Government's legislation to create a public trusteeship was swiftly passed in the Canadian Parliament without a single dissenting vote, and the trusteeship proclaimed a few days later. The American SIU promptly boycotted Canadian ships in United States ports. Stern notes were dispatched from Ottawa to Washington, demanding that the Administration use its authority to enable Canadian shipping to ply freely on the Lakes. There were assurances that the Administration would do what it could. But it did not seem able to do very much. The Leader of the Opposition put his finger on the difficulty. "There is no help from the United States," Mr. Diefenbaker declared, "because Mr. Kennedy needs votes." No Canadian, least of all the prairie wheat farmer anxious to move his crop to Eastern Europe, was ready to stand patiently by until after November 1964. But it was not easy to see what alternative he had.

Resources of the mind

The depth of Canadian concern on any national issue may easily be measured by the number of Royal Commissions dealing with its subject. By this standard it is evident that on one issue Canadians feel very deeply indeed: whether there can survive a distinctively Canadian culture in North America. In the past decade and a half, no fewer than four Royal Commissions have been appointed to investigate various aspects of this problem. The Royal Commission on National Development in the Arts, Letters and Science (the Massey Commission) reported in 1951; the Royal Commission on Broadcasting (the Fowler Commission) reported in 1957; the Royal Commission on Publications (the O'Leary Commission) reported in 1961; the Royal Commission on Bi-Culturalism (the

Dunton-Laurendeau Commission) was appointed in 1963 and its report is not yet complete.

Through their reports and appendices there runs a common set of assumptions. A nation (they all suppose) worthy of the name is not just a political expression but an identifiable and distinctive way of life, a people possessing a culture of their own, a style of national existence. Canada has the capacity for becoming and remaining a nation in this sense. Their most provocative assumption on the reports is their central assumption that Canada's capacity for meaningful nationhood is somehow being thwarted and undermined by the proximity and potency of the cultural output of the United States. Thus the Massey Commissioners express resentment at the "vast and disproportionate amount of material coming from a single *alien* source" [my italics]. The Fowler Commissioners remark that "the dangers to Canadian national identity are much greater from the good American programmes than from their poor or clumsy productions." The O'Leary Commissioners observe that "the tremendous expansion of communications in the United States has given that nation the world's most penetrating and effective apparatus for the transmission of ideas. Canada, more than any other country, is naked to that force, exposed unceasingly to a vast network of communications which reaches to every corner of our land; American words, images and print—the good, the bad, the indifferent—batter unrelentingly at our eyes and ears." And the Dunton-Laurendeau Commissioners are almost sure to say, in so many words, that one of the most compelling reasons why Canadians and *Canadiens* should stop quarreling with each other and get on with the job of nation-building is to protect their own cultures from the cultural imperialism of the United States.

Throughout, too, there runs a common remedy. State intervention, in one form or another, is essential to create and support a countervailing cultural force to the unrelenting flow of Americana across the border. The Massey Report recommended increased governmental philanthropy in all aspects of the arts. The Fowler Report recommended increased radio and television programming through the publicly-owned Canadian Broadcasting Corporation and prescribed that a minimum proportion of the programming of the privately-owned stations should be produced in Canada and about Canada. The O'Leary Report recommended the imposition of certain protective devices designed to deflect advertising revenue from so-called "Canadian editions" of American magazines (notably *Time* and *Reader's Digest*) to genuinely Canadian publications. Legislation on these matters was acted upon by the Canadian governments of the day.

Cultural protectionism

Canada's cultural protectionism may properly appear to a United States administration as a problem on the agenda of Canadian-American relations to be dealt with in intergovernmental discussion. It is known, indeed, that President Eisenhower took up with Canadian Ministers the proposed tax on the advertising revenue of "Canadian Editions" (reportedly on behalf and at the instigation of his powerful friend, Henry Luce). That such a technique, given the Canadian mood, is likely to be counter-productive is another matter. There is at least an issue. Private interests in the United States are adversely affected by Canadian policies; and the United States government, like any self-respecting government, must do what it can to protect its own citizens from injuries unjustly inflicted.

But on the Canadian side there is no such issue. What Canadians choose to regard as the cultural activities of the United States are in fact the product of the private sector, and very largely involuntary. No Voice of America beams propaganda in Canada's direction—though Canadians might be culturally better off if it did. Nor is the private sector in any sense a creature of the Administration. Whatever the faults of the manipulators of the communications systems, pandering to the United States government is not among them. They go their own way unmindful of the feeble surveillance of the Federal Communications Commission; in their pursuit of sensationalism and the sordid side of life they are cheerfully unhampered by true patriot love. It is even more incongruous to see the private sector as the bully of the Administration, forcing it to retail their shoddy wares abroad.

Canadians must educate themselves about these things. They must learn, as well, not to impute to the source of supply the faults of the consumer. If their national taste has been dragged to the level of the gutter by the culture of the gutter, it is not because of external influence but through a sickness in their own souls. Were they cut off from the grosser output of Madison Avenue and Beverly Hills by some Iron Curtain of their own, they would quickly generate their own indigenous sources of corruption—just as the peoples of Eastern Europe have done, in spite of the ruthless and callow puritanism of their commissars of culture. Fortunately for Canadians, they have as yet no Ministry of Public Enlightenment; their commissars are confined to the Ministry of National Revenue where, in the humble guise of customs officials, they keep their countrymen free from the moral taint of exposure to the works of D. H. Lawrence or Jean Genêt.

It is really up to Canadians themselves to seek out and hold to the fine and shifting line between a nationalism that is constructive and a nationalism that is neurotic—neurotic in the precise clinical sense of becoming a prey to irrational fears to such an extent that their own health and happiness are blighted. Luckily for them, for all of North America, there are a few among them who want to share, not to divide, the continent's resources of the mind. "What we need," the historian Frank Underhill has written, "is closer contact with [its] finest expressions. . . . The fear that what will result from such contact will be our own absorption is pure defeatism. The Americans are now mature enough to have come through this adolescent phase of believing that the way to become mature is to cut yourself off from the older people who are more mature than you are. It is about time that we grew out of it also." Amen to that.

Good Neighbours Make Good Fences

Canada and the United States, by a curious coincidence, are encountering at the same time the supreme crisis of their respective modern histories. In the United States, the critical issue is whether all Americans, particularly Negro Americans, are to share fully in the promise of their Constitution. In Canada, the critical issue is whether all Canadians, and particularly French-speaking Canadians, consider their country worth keeping.

The United States crisis: race

The race question in the United States is crucially important for American foreign policy. The leader of liberally minded societies confronts the totalitarian challenge. The outcome of that confrontation now depends less on piling up military force than on whether the ideals and institutions of the West command the respect of newly emergent peoples in Asia, Latin America, Africa. Liberal democracy will be judged not by the number of cars in each garage, still less by the number of its astronauts upon the moon, but by the extent to which American Negroes can attain by peaceful means the equal status to which they are entitled, not only in the law of the land but in the hearts of their countrymen.

Whether the United States emerges creditably from its crisis, or plunges once again into civil war, is of supreme importance to Canadians as well as to Americans. But the racial policies of the United States government are not now the legitimate concern of a Canadian government. Nor will they become its legitimate concern, except in the unlikely event of a relapse into repression. The Canadian government and the Canadian people play their part best by putting their own house in order. There is much to keep them preoccupied.

The Canadian crisis: nationhood

Canada's crisis is not a crisis of race. It is a crisis of nationhood. An important body of French-speaking Canadian opinion has become dissatisfied with the conditions of its participation in the experiment of Confederation. The extent of its alienation first became apparent to the nation at large in 1962. In the General Election of that year, the voters of Quebec expressed their alienation by voting in large numbers for a fiery demagogue who made no secret of his admiration for the methods of Mussolini and Hitler. "You do not have to understand Social Credit to vote for it," Réal Caouette told his followers, and he urged them to vote Social Credit because "you have nothing to lose." Many agreed with him. Their desertion of their traditional political allegiance did as much as anything else to make English-speaking Canadians conscious of the resentments and aspirations of their French-speaking compatriots. It helped to make them aware that these are widespread and mostly justified, and induced a struggle, in a sort of enfeebled desperation, to make amends.

Such amends as they have been able and willing to make come too late to arrest the growth of a powerful movement demanding the separation of French Canada from the rest of Canada. The movement reaches back to the Great Depression, when a handful of intellectuals and racial nationalists dreamed their dreams of *Laurentie*—a French-language republican redoubt sheltering within its independent frontiers a community secure from the buffetings of an alien world. Today's separatist does not have to dream. He has, whatever his opponents may say, a workable alternative. If Cyprus or Malta, Chad or the Niger, can make a go of self-determination, why not Quebec, far more populous and wealthy, infinitely more experienced politically? Some say an independent Quebec would not be viable. But viability in the modern states-system is the condition of being treated by its members as if you were viable. And an independent Quebec would not go friendless into the world.

This crisis of nationhood presents to a Prime Minister of Canada an issue transcending all others in urgency and importance. For many years it was his main concern so to conduct his countrymen's affairs that there would continue to be two sovereign governments in North America, not one. Today his main concern is that there continue to be two sovereign governments, not three. No Canadian Prime Minister, least of all an English-speaking Prime Minister, wants to be remembered as the man who presided over the liquidation of Confederation.

A Canadian government, apart from putting its own house in order, cannot do much to affect the outcome of the racial crisis in the United States. But an American government will have much to do with the outcome of the crisis of nationhood in Canada. If there are not to be three sovereign governments in North America, the most powerful of North American governments must emphasize, even exaggerate, the sovereignty of its neighbour. Quebec (for reasons suggested elsewhere in this volume) is of all the Provinces most fearful of *americanization*. To the extent that it values Confederation, it is as a bulwark against those forces from the United States —political, economic, perhaps above all cultural—perceived as threats to the integrity of the French *esprit* in North America. If by capitulating to the logic of integration the Canadian government no longer provides safe shelter, Quebec is likely to conclude that there is more safety in independence than in Confederation.

The international vs. the neighbourly

If the Canadian-American relationship is to flourish to the mutual benefit of its partners, it will be because statesmen of both countries resist the temptation, to which they have yielded in the past, of believing their politics to be neighbourly rather than international. They must realize that the two nations of North America are of the states-system, not beyond and above it, and shape their policies accordingly. President Johnson, with the best intentions in the world, observed in his first official reference to the Canadian-American relationship that "Canada is such a close neighbor and such a good neighbor that we always have plenty of problems there. They are kind of like problems in the hometown." They are kind of not like that at all. They are the problems not of neighbours but of friendly foreign powers.

What is really required is a certain reserve, a sense of live and let live, even of aloofness on occasion, in the treatment of the smaller country by the larger. "Good fences," American leaders are fond of quoting on their Canadian visits, "make good neighbors." They could usefully remember that good neighbours make good fences. One at least has remembered. "If we keep our distance," George Kennan has declared, "and concede to them the privilege of their privacy and their differentness, as we would like to have it conceded to us, being prepared to reserve judgment on that which we cannot understand and which need not concern us, I can see no reason why a satisfactory relationship should not be established." It is true that Mr. Kennan was speaking of the relationship between the United States and the Soviet Union. But his prescription will contribute no less admirably to the good health of the relationship between the United States and Canada.

John W. Holmes 

4

The Relationship in Alliance and in World Affairs

The good neighbour policy between the United States and Canada remains a good policy, but it is no longer enough. To accept without tantrums litigation over frontiers and seaways is the first principle of civilized relations. In the present age, however, the disputes which involve the two governments and raise the popular hackles are as likely to be over China as over water levels, and their mutual endeavours as likely to be undertaken in Asia as in North America. Relations between the two countries are not only bilateral but also multilateral; they are not only two countries which share a continent, but also a major and a middle power in world affairs, acting both as partners and as independent entities in international politics, deeply involved in the security and stability of the world at large, engrossed individually and collectively in diplomacy. It is with the nature of the relationship on the world scene, in the United Nations, in NATO, in the turbulent diplomacy of our times that this essay is concerned. These involvements have added an important dimension to a simple international life when we were

---

JOHN WENDELL HOLMES *is president of the Canadian Institute of International Affairs. For many years he was a member of the Department of External Affairs—serving as Assistant Under Secretary of State in that Department from 1953 to 1960. Mr. Holmes was Acting Permanent Representative of Canada to the United Nations, 1950-51, and for two years was on the staff of the National Defence College.*

isolated not only from other continents but also from each other. To differentiate the multilateral from the bilateral, and matters political from matters economic, is difficult. Nevertheless, because bilateral economic and defence issues are emphasized elsewhere in this volume, the focus here is mainly on the multilateral and the political.

A Bilateral Alliance with a Multilateral Framework

Today the major premise in the relationship between the United States and Canada in international politics is the fact that they are formal allies. This fact is, however, both so recent and so pervasive that its implications are not yet fully comprehended.

Before Pearl Harbour the two countries, although associated in a common military effort in 1917-18, were at no time "military allies." Common interests and mutual pressures had affected each country's independent formulation of its foreign policies. In 1921, for example, Canada, in deference to strong American feelings, opposed the renewal of the Anglo-Japanese Alliance. Because they were not acknowledged allies, however, there was not the expectation which now exists that they should follow common policies. The Ogdensburg Agreement of 1940 established what was intended as a permanent military partnership, but this was part of a broader wartime coalition dedicated to the defeat of a specific enemy. Within the coalition Canada, as one of the leading lesser powers, pursued its own point of view while learning to accept decisions which were usually the consensus of the great powers. In the establishment of the terms of peace and the constitution of the United Nations, Canada was as unfettered in its policies as any member of the association, finding its collaborators for the most part among the other middle powers. When the United Nations was transformed from a wartime coalition into an association of diverse states, the wartime team dissolved. During the latter years of the war and particularly in the common effort after the war to aid the stricken Europeans, Canada had been acting in concert, of course, with the United States, achieving thereby a national self-confidence, a sense of partnership, and at the same time new independent-mindedness.

In the creation of the North Atlantic Treaty Organization in 1949 a new team was formed. Canada and the United States became bound together within a military alliance. It was for the two countries a tighter bond than ever before because this alliance incorporated the idea of common aims in foreign policy and an obligation to consult with a view to reaching agreement. The supreme military importance of the United States in NATO reinforced the special obligation of a lesser ally to act only after taking fully into account American policies and interests. Canada entered into this military alliance with its powerful neighbour in association with other nations and in particular with the two powers to which it was most closely tied by history, Britain and France. The fact that the United States-Canada alliance was inaugurated as a multilateral association and has continued in that framework is basic to an understanding of the obligations involved and the attitudes of both parties to those obligations. Canadians prefer to see them as obligations to a collectivity rather than to a single ally, although they do hanker perversely after a special relationship with the United States nonetheless. Americans, for the most part, see their relations with Canada as similar to those with their other allies not only in NATO but also in SEATO and the OAS, while expecting nevertheless a special brand of fidelity from next-door neighbours who are blood relations.

The bilateral aspects of the United States-Canada military alliance, which had been developing in practice for a decade, were made more precise in 1957 by the arrangements for collaboration in NORAD (North American Air Defence). Although NORAD undeniably drew Canada into closer involvement with the consequences of United States foreign policies, or at least formally organized the involvement, the implications for Canadian foreign policy were tacit, acknowledged more readily in the chanceries than expounded to the public. The Canadian attitude to the implications of NORAD on its alignment is still left, perhaps deliberately, ambivalent to allow more flexibility for ad hoc interpretations. It is not even certain whether NORAD is to be viewed as a sector within the NATO framework. Although Canadian military leaders, like their American colleagues, have minimized the sector concept in order to avoid interference from NATO, the present political leaders of Canada have always favoured the view that NORAD was a bilateral arrangement within a multilateral structure.

The Canadian alternative of nonalignment

The analysis in this paper is based on the premise of the alliance rather than of Canadian nonalignment because there is little likelihood of the latter's being accepted by a governing majority of

Canadians. It does however, remain an alternative in the back of the Canadian mind. The deciding argument is not that nonalignment is illogical or unworthy but that it is improbable for an unneutral people. It is difficult to believe that Canadians, closely bound not only to the interests but also to the thought-processes of Americans and the European allies, would set themselves categorically apart from the countries with which they are historically and intellectually allied. Practical calculations are also important. Whereas the United States government would be reluctant to take arbitrary action if Canadian foreign policy diverged sharply, it is doubtful if the Canadian will could stand up to the fury of a hostile Congress and the animosity of Washington officials, with their power to strike back in anger on Canada's exposed economic front. The need for a benevolent Congress as well as a sweetly disposed Administration keeps Canadian foreign policy from straying too far from that of its ally. Canadians assume, furthermore, that although they are unlikely to have a decisive influence on Western strategy, they are more likely to be felt inside the Alliance than out in the cold.

The weight of these factors could, however, change. As a result of missile development, less importance may be attached to Canadian contributions to the defence both of the United States and Western Europe. The increasing concentration of Western power and authority in the hands of the United States, however inevitable, encourages independence and a measure of disengagement on the part of the lesser partners—especially if the inclination in Soviet-American relations is towards two-power negotiations at the Summit. A détente with the Soviet Union might diminish the importance attached to NATO, reduce the significance of "alignment" or "nonalignment" and weaken the argument for Canada's deference to the United States in the determination of its foreign policy, although a détente based on equilibrium between the blocs would not in fact justify the disintegration of NATO.

As the present association is based not merely on common fear but also on a recognition of common interests and attitudes, the Canadian-United States partnership is unlikely to fly apart merely because the Russians reduce the pressure. For present purposes it is safe to assume that the military alliance will continue to be the determining factor. Some consideration to so-called "neutralist" thinking in Canada is essential, however, because it leavens the attitudes of many who would not go so far as nonalignment. As one perceptive Canadian, F. H. Soward observed:

This yearning for neutralism reflects above all the helpless feeling of a people who see their world dominated by superpowers equipped with dreadful and expensive weapons over which they have not the slightest control.

The limits of the alliance

The political implications of the military alliance between the United States and Canada are not clear. Any attempt to define them formally would be not only futile but injudicious. Debate over abstract rights and duties would create tensions that prevent accommodation. The occasional rhetorical interpretation by statesmen is useful as a guidepost or a reaffirmation of common purpose, but the application must be left to political leaders who can adapt them to the military necessities of each situation and the current temper of their respective countries.

The alliance itself is spelt out in no single treaty but is to be deduced from the Ogdensburg Agreement, the North Atlantic Treaty, NORAD, numerous military arrangements and bilateral agreements. In its political implications it is not universal; it is more binding in some areas than others. The engagement to align policies is clearer in the North Atlantic and West Europe, where the two countries are united in a consultative alliance, than in the Pacific or Latin America, where the United States is bound in alliances to which Canada is not a party. There is no sense of obligation to common policies towards China or Cuba comparable to the contract to harmonize policies over East Germany. This is not to say that the two allies have no mutual obligations in other than Atlantic areas. These, however, are based not on treaty undertakings but on a recognition of fundamental interests which leaves more latitude in interpretation. They are based also on a recognition that if United States policy towards China or Cuba should culminate in an air attack on the United States, Canada would be involved through NORAD. The specific commitment in the North Atlantic is traceable to historical factors; it reflects a fundamental assessment not that the two have more permanent common interests there than anywhere else but rather that in the postwar years Europe was where the situation seemed most critical and where collaboration had become customary. The security of the world being interlocked as it is in the nuclear age, it is unwise to isolate regions where mutual interests are believed stronger than in others. The threat to Canada as well as the United States can be ignited in Central Africa, Northern Brazil, or Sarawak as readily as in Berlin, even though Canadian military forces are not poised for immediate involvement in those areas. It is essential, therefore, to comprehend what the United States-Canada alliance involves that is basic and deeper than the explicit and immediate commitments.

The United States role as "champion" of the Alliance

Canada's relationship to the United States in world affairs is special but not entirely unique; it is basically the same as that of other "Western countries." The common frontier is elemental in their bilateral relations, but in the multilateral relations of the two countries it is less significant than is usually assumed. One might think of some last stand in which the United States and Canada huddled together on the North American continent, but this is not today's working hypothesis. The peace and happiness of Canadians depend on the maintenance of a balance of power and the prevalence of order on the whole planet in the same way as do the peace and happiness of Belgians or Australians. They have the same dependence on the power of the United States, the same common interest in the preservation of that power and the maintenance of its prestige.

The United States is not so much the ally of Canada and other countries within its "power cluster" as their champion. The resources of the United States and its lesser allies are so disproportionate that the military contributions of the latter, except in bases, are marginal; they are valued more for political than military reasons. The "champion's role" of the United States is a triple one: it is able and disposed, if not necessarily committed, to defend its allies from attack; it maintains its end of the duel of deterrence with the communist world; it carries on the dialogue with the Soviet Union through which we all hope to move towards a better structure of order. It is the common aim to break out of this transitional stage into a more stable world order in which right and justice are less directly associated with pressure and compromise. In the meantime, Canada and other middle powers must bear in mind constantly the significance of American "championing" strength for whatever stability they have in the world today.

The real nature of the alliance relationship is obscured by the rhetoric of "free and equal partnership." A further reason for obscurity is the reluctance of the United States to assert a paramount position for itself—for sound diplomatic reasons and because of its disinclination to assume more of the global burden. By its actions, of course, it does make clear its view of the relationship to its allies, as for instance in its unhesitating adherence to its own policy in the Cuban crisis or its determination to pursue limited talks with the Russians in spite of the reservations of Paris and Bonn. The United States would prefer to act in concert with its allies, but if it can't it may be expected to act anyway. The allies are valuable to the United States even if the Alliance is in some respects a mirage. The United States administration is strengthened both in dealing with Congress and in appealing to world opinion by appearing as one member of a strong association. And whatever the military realities, the West is politically stronger if it can appear as a mutual-benefit association.

It is in this larger context of ambivalent general alliance that the bilateral relationship must be seen. A sensible approach to the difficult questions of community and independence in foreign policy must be based on a conception of the world at large, not merely this continent. Canada can rarely claim special influence on the policies of Washington on the argument of its proximity, although the dependence of the United States on Canadian defence installations and facilities may outlast its dependence on countries overseas. Relying on the inescapable commitment of the United States to defend all of North America, Canada has often displayed less timidity than more distant allies in differing with United States policy. The alignment of Canada with forces hostile to the United States would, of course, present to that country a far greater threat than even Cuba, but the blackmailing advantages this situation presents to Canada have always been offset by the reasonable confidence Americans have had that Canadians, however "bloody-minded," would never turn malevolent. Blackmail, like deterrence, must be credible. Canadians in turn have long since tacitly recognized that the United States in the last resort would not tolerate too close a Canadian association with their enemies.

The Canadian role: support without satellitism

In the enormous dialogue into which the world may be moving, one voice may be better than several for purposes both of strategy and negotiation. The illusion that this can be a clear, firm. single-minded voice emanating collectively from NATO dies hard, especially in Washington. The United States now has the responsibility almost alone to match actions and words, calculate threats or promises. It has the specialized information and the expertise against which allies find difficulty even in maintaining an argument. Canada and the other allies must, therefore, be reluctant to weaken the

American position by adopting variant policies or by criticizing American policy shrilly whether they are entirely satisfied with it or not. This is a fact of the age which Canadians must accept, distasteful though it may seem when stated bluntly. It is, however, only one fact in the paradox.

The logic of a satellite posture for Canada is as clear as the logic of theoretical neutrality and it suffers from the same disadvantage; it is incompatible with public attitudes. Nations persist and cannot be wished away. Their pride and sense of responsibility are as much a force for good in the world as for ill. The West Europeans chafe within the Alliance and yet in some ways the position of Canada is harder. The European countries have national identities and traditional associations which abide even though their relative power declines. Canada, more obviously—by the map at least—a candidate for satellite status, is under constant pressure to reassure the world at large as well as its own public that it is not the docile neighbour they assume it to be. Conformity to United States foreign policy can, therefore, be even more politically painful for a Canadian government than for that of, say, Holland or the Philippines. It is futile to dismiss this sort of thing as childish nationalism out of tune with the times. A sense of national purpose is as essential for a middle power as a great power, and lofty admonitions from the United States, which has long cultivated in its citizens a more intense and conformist nationalism than has Canada, are, in the American phrase, "counter-productive." Resistance to United States pressure (which is *not* properly called anti-Americanism) is endemic in a nation composed, as Canada has been by history, of those Americans who have not wanted to join the United States. For the foreseeable future, therefore, it should be assumed that Canadians are unlikely to accept anything like a doctrine of automatic conformity as the basis of their foreign policy.

The Cuban Crisis of October 1962, for example, did not prove that the allies would seek agreement and act in concert in a moment of crisis. It proved simply that if the United States challenged a communist opponent, the other allies would be likely to recognize a fundamental interest in supporting their "champion" right or wrong. It is significant that neither Canada nor most of the other NATO countries, although they supported the United States when it was challenged, has felt compelled subsequently to alter its policy of diplomatic and commercial relations with Cuba to conform with that of the United States.

The fallacy of total alignment

The fallacy of the argument for the undeviating alignment of allies lies in an oversimplified view of the world and the forces loose in it. It assumes that the world is divided into two camps and that nothing else matters except the struggle for dominance between them. It may well be true that the need to maintain Western strength against the communist threat is the most important issue and the one which should in the end determine the policies of our two countries. To assume, however, that any single frame of reference could guide all the decisions of allies in foreign policy is to be guilty of a Marxist type of heresy. The upheaval involved in the transition of an imperial world to a world of self-governing units makes the factors much more complex. So does the struggle for trade and markets, which cuts across the political and military alignments.

The bipolarization of the world into which we have been forced is a dangerous and undesirable condition which we should seek to transcend as soon as possible. The cracking of the monolithic structure of the communist world presents opportunities for exploration. The deliberate effort of the United States to foster a centre of power in a unified Europe, whether futile or not, is another effort to break through the limited framework in which we have been congealed for too many years, to loosen international society, and by permitting more freedom of national expression reduce the danger of explosion. Close alignment and the unity of the West have been necessary principles and cannot lightly be abandoned so long as the East is united. Nevertheless, the world will be better off when the international political situation is such that we can safely abandon them. Just as within the state it is dangerous to have certain regions or interests set in permanent confrontation, so too the world community would be healthier if the combinations of states could be more fluid. For the United States and Canada close alignment is still imperative, requiring the willingness of Canada to accept American leadership, but it need not be assumed that this alignment is an end in itself and our single aim closer—let alone total—alignment. There is no good argument for deliberate disunity; the pursuit of agreement should be eternal. The aim, however, should be a world in which close neighbours can pursue more freely than they dare at present their separate functions in the world. Our purpose, as U Thant has said, is to make the world safe for diversity.

The Role of the Middle Power

The argument for variations in the foreign policies of the two countries is not that this is unavoidable but that it is desirable, that it is in the interest not only of Canada but of the United States and the world at large. Great powers and lesser powers have different functions to perform to keep the world stable. The role of a great power, or a super-power, in the present state of disorder is usually well defined. The role of the middle power is more difficult to define.

When originally used towards the end of the last War the term "middle power" was associated with the so-called "functional theory" of which Canada was a principal advocate. According to this theory great powers were recognized as having special responsibility in security matters. It was argued, however, that countries like Canada and Australia which had carried a fair share of the fighting, and also countries like Sweden, India, or Brazil, which were expected to play a considerable part in economic and diplomatic activities, ought not to be equated in international organizations with very small countries. The patterns would vary in accordance with the function of the organization. The great powers might not have the same special position in economic questions as they were accorded in questions involving military matters. Canada, because of its role with Britain and the United States in developing atomic power, became the one non-great power with permanent membership on the United Nations Atomic Energy Commission. This special status was later accorded Canada on successor bodies dealing more generally with disarmament. It gave Canada for many years a position in great power circles which may have fostered an exaggerated idea of its place in the world. The concept of states divided not only into alliances but also in classes as large, middle, or small powers comes easily to those accustomed to think of states in terms of distinct functions.

One of the most useful functions middle powers have performed in helping to keep the peace has been as participants in international undertakings to maintain truces. Inevitably, therefore, the ambiguous connotation of mediation, of a middle position, has crept into the term "middle power." Countries like Norway, Ireland, and Tunisia became as much "middle powers" as the original roster of somewhat larger states. As a mediatory-minded middle power Canada has had more experience than perhaps any other country. In addition to providing personnel for United Nations commissions in Kashmir, Palestine, Lebanon, and most recently in West Irian, Yemen, and Cyprus, Canada has played a major role in staffing the Supervisory Commissions in Indo-China and the United Nations Emergency Force in the Gaza Strip, with a technically important but less populous role in the Congo. Since the time of the Suez Crisis it has been assumed that, the principal purpose of such operations being to prevent the great powers from being involved, none of them should be invited to participate.

Military involvement inevitably means involvement in the diplomacy of the areas in dispute. Both inside the United Nations and outside it (Laos and Vietnam, for example) Canada has been drawn into an intermediary role which requires not neutrality as it is usually understood but a certain impartiality or detachment as far as the particular dispute is concerned. This position has given a certain style to Canadian diplomacy, a knack of brokerage in evidence behind the scenes on Palestine, Indonesia, and even the South Tyrol, and, within Commonwealth circles, on issues between "colonialists" and "anti-colonialists." The role has suited the Canadian tradition, which thrives on compromise, and appealed to the Canadian imagination. The Canadian armed services recognize continuing commitments of this kind, and the Canadian public has taken pride in the role because it provides a unique and significant function in the world, a function that is different in kind from, but in no sense inimical to, that of its great neighbour. To be different but not inimical fits the Canadian vocation.

Dilemmas of middle-power diplomacy

It is argued, therefore, that Canada and the United States should seek a partnership in world politics not in the illusion of equality but as a great power and a middle power performing in the international community unique functions which are complementary. The theory is not difficult to enunciate; it is a deduction from recent history rather than merely an intellectual idea. As such it is a useful definition of aspirations to help both countries see the way. Like all definitions, it is too neat for a disorderly world, but it has the virtue that it suggests not only what to strive for but also what not to expect.

The basic advantage of this concept is that it permits disagreement while still providing the opportunity for collaboration in good causes. Here, however, it is necessary to keep one's feet on the ground lest national gamesmen be too giddily attracted by the possibilities of collusively assigning special roles to each other in team plays. This kind of oversophisticated diplomacy rarely comes off.

In fulfilling its complementary role, Canada must convince the world at large that it is genuinely independent in the formulation of its policy and not acting as a "front" for a great power ally. It must do so not merely for its self-esteem but for the effectiveness of its diplomacy. This problem was faced by Canada when it took a leading part in establishing the UNEF at the time of the Suez Crisis in 1956. It was only by submitting proof from the Canadian record and calling on the witness of friends that Canada was able to convince the Egyptians that it was acting in good faith and not seeking merely to promote the interests of Britain and France in the guise of U.N. action. As a Canadian general was to command and Canadian forces to play a major part, it was crucial to the success of the whole delicate affair that Canada be trusted by a majority in the Assembly. Canada was taking the lead on its own initiative but with the support of Mr. Dulles because he recognized that there was a better chance to get majority support if the middle power rather than the great power took the lead on the floor. Canada, however, had to make clear that it was no agent of the Americans. Even though awareness that the United States would support the enterprise was decisive in persuading the Assembly to take the Canadian proposal seriously, an acknowledged American initiative would inevitably look like a Cold War scheme from which the nonaligned would abstain. It was well known that Canada had on occasions in and out of the United Nations differed with the United States out of conviction and pursued an independent course. Paradoxically, it was recognized also, even by countries which could not themselves support the United States out loud, that Canada, however independent its actions, was unlikely to sponsor a proposal unless it was convinced the proposal was not contrary to the fundamental interests of the Western powers.

The problem for the smaller power is to remain loyal to its obligations to the large ally while giving constant proof that its policies are not made by the ally. It is not always easy for the United States to understand that an ally which acts independently and seems troublesome but nevertheless respects the fundamental community of interest can be a more useful ally than one which is too docile to be respected in international society.

"Influence" within an Unequal Partnership

The concept of separate functions does not answer the eternal question of how the smaller ally gets an effective "say" on issues of common concern. How can not only Canada but also larger powers like Britain and France exert influence on the decisive power, the United States? Raymond Aron, speaking of what he called "the old quarrel concerning consultation with allies, as distinguished from merely informing them," has said, "This, however, is a demand which is as difficult to satisfy as it is to reject." If we must renounce as unachievable the concept of a common policy for the whole Alliance of the West, can all major decisions simply be left to the United States? This might be a possibility if the other countries were prepared to recognize that crucial decisions were beyond them and declare their intention of dedicating themselves to useful and independent effort in the 90 per cent of diplomacy and international politics that does not involve grand strategy—although it shapes the world we live in—trade and aid and health and most things, social, economic, and political, on the agenda of United Nations bodies. This would be an easier course for Canada than for the proud nations of Western Europe or distant allies less intimately bound to American security, who are inevitably less disposed to entrust their security entirely to Washington. No nation, however, can in practice abdicate all hope of participation in the decisions which determine the future of the world. Even lesser allies must somehow try to exert influence on American policy—or at least seem to. To do so is a declared part of Canadian government policy under any regime, but the fulfillment of this aim is difficult and frustrating, not so much because of American intransigence as because in today's world some hundred nations, whether friends, antagonists, or nonaligned, all want to have an impact on American policy.

Such influence cannot be allotted in mathematical terms or with priorities—Britain having, for instance, a right to one fifth of a decision, France, when it behaves, one sixth, and Canada one fifteenth. Policy is not composed that way. American policy is composed not by computers but by human beings who might be swayed by General de Gaulle, Walter Lippmann, or a chance remark by the Nepalese Chargé d'Affaires. It is a rough principle that in the formulation of anything as serious as Western policies good ideas tend to rise and bad ideas sink—notwithstanding the obvious fact that the allies have embraced some pretty dubious proposals. If a middle power like Canada wishes to be heard, it must think with a broad world view, not just from a narrowly Canadian angle.

For exposed allies like Germany the problem of influence is not only that of shaping wise policy for the Alliance as a whole but also of protecting the special, on-the-spot, security interests of the nation as they see them. On most issues of world order and security, however, it is hard to distinguish specially Canadian national interests that need to be guarded against an American disposition to bargain them away. Canada is concerned with using its influence to keep American policy on lines which Canadians happen to favour. Canada has from time to time urged the United States to shift its course over China or Korea or nuclear tests, not because a Canadian interest is involved but because Canadians think the world would be better off if things moved in a certain direction. In such circumstances it is harder to get a hearing than if one could plead a threat to one's territory, security, or income. On economic questions the situation may be quite different. Canada holds, for example, that its commercial interests are threatened by the rigidity of American attitudes on trade in nonstrategic materials with communist countries and also by United States policy, for political as well as economic reasons, in distributing agricultural surpluses under PL-480 to the disruption of Canadian trade.

Difficulties in the dialogue of the Alliance

A super-power, particularly a complicated democracy such as the United States, has a colossal job making up its own mind, and when it has done so it is hard to shake. To reach a decision on China, Vietnam, or Berlin the State Department, White House, Pentagon, C.I.A., other agencies, and Congressional leaders must first negotiate among themselves, a process which can be protracted. The result is viewed as the end-product of a complicated, delicate negotiation each phase of which has involved compromise and which can be altered or even reopened only at great risk of bringing down the edifice. Under these circumstances, less deference might be paid to the view of a neighbour than to that of one of the Washington powers. Because such intragovernmental negotiations are delicate, it is rarely possible for allies even to be kept informed of how things are going, although the State Department, knowing the views of allies, does its best to see that attention is paid to them. When Canada was a member of the five-power United Nations Sub-

Committee on Disarmament its position was peculiarly frustrating. It was unwilling to act irresponsibly on its own in matters involving world security, but it was unable to have effective discussions of policy with the United States. The willingness of Washington to discuss was not in doubt, but the preliminary battle of Washington would inevitably result in an agreed American policy on the eve of the opening of the sessions of the Sub-Committee, leaving no time for comment, certainly not for substantial revision.

There is no need, however, for Canadians to be defeatist. The process of affecting American policy is baffling but not impossible. Canadians and the other allies can and do have an impact when they are able to inject sound ideas, directly or indirectly, into the process at an early stage.

Defence talk is not cheap

The smaller ally faces another serious problem in maintaining a meaningful dialogue with the United States on strategic policies. Americans, with a somewhat more categorical attitude towards facts and an infinitely vaster establishment for accumulating them, tend to turn bilateral discussions into briefing sessions in which Canadians are awed into sceptical silence. When NORAD was established, it was recognized that as Canada would inevitably be involved in wars resulting from American policies, it had a special right to share in the discussion of policy. If the special arrangements for such discussions have been less effective than intended, the reason is not so much the lack of American good intentions as the disproportion between the apparatus of the participants.

The enormous fact and thought-collecting establishment which stands behind American policy-making has become something of an obstacle to discussion with its allies. It is, of course, open to others to reproduce this process in their own countries, but anything comparable would be beyond Canada's resources even if the job were tackled more diligently than at present. The kind of specialization in which the United States indulges, from Cambridge, Massachusetts to Santa Monica, California, drawing talent not only from the United States but also from abroad, has accentuated the imbalance in the allied relationship. The foreigner can be smothered by massive detail and his case overwhelmed by an array of accumulated positions on all the permutations of conflict and by conclusions about the expected behaviour of all the powers—his own included. Most serious of all, he is presented with security reports which he has no means of checking or matching. Since the days of the Korean War he has had to preserve scepticism about the relationship between the facts in the security report and the policy which the United States is asking him to support. Frustrated by this onesided dialogue, the foreigner is tempted into obscurantism by deploring the gigantic American effort to organize both information and ratiocination. Many foreigners do have serious doubts about the intellectual processes involved, and there is a danger of a widening rift between the mental processes of Americans and their allies. Canadians, in this dialogue, are tempted either to retreat into stubborn doubt or give up, forgetting that they have their own compensating advantages in the compactness of the Canadian policy-forming procedures. To accuse the United States of arrogance in the intellectual relationship would be unfair; this enormous effort had its roots in American humility and a determination to base policy on knowledge rather than ignorance. In the result, however, there is a self-confidence which discourages the dialogue with allies and the sharing of burdens, both of which the United States is so obviously anxious to promote.

Americans might well ask why this Canadian preoccupation with influence. Is it a neurotic compulsion to cut a figure in the world? To write it off as anti-Americanism is to pursue a form of obscurantism which has too long bedevilled American thinking about its allies. The insistence on an effective, independent voice is based not on distrust of the United States as a benign and intelligent entity but on scepticism about the supreme wisdom of any country or any person alone. Even a country as powerful as the United States and as well educated, it is assumed, needs the kind of perspective that can come only from outsiders who are friends and allies as well. There is also the undeniable compulsion of a people, themselves politically aware and educated, to affect the policy which affects them through the only instrument available to them, their national government. Because the extent of the influence of any middle power in a very busy world is inevitably small, there is bound to be frustration and impatience. The fact that many Canadians, and at times the Canadian government, overestimate their importance in the scheme of things does not mean that there is not a calculable, sensible influence which Canada can exert in the alliance; which, indeed, it must exert if the United States-Canadian relationship is to contribute something more than mere geography to the society of nations and to the larger alliances.

THE TRIANGLE AND THE LINCHPIN FALLACY

One of the most obfuscating theories about Canada's role in the world is that it is the "interpreter" between Britain and the United States, the "linchpin," as Sir Winston Churchill, among others, has said. Even the metaphor is misguided. A linchpin holds a wheel on to a chassis, and the spirit of the symbolism would be spoiled by an effort to identify whether Britain or the United States was the wheel or the carriage. This idea must have been conceived by Canadians groping for some rationalization of their frustrating position in the world, and by Britons and Americans as a post-prandial sop to a friend. During World War II when the phrase was most popular, Messrs. Churchill and Roosevelt, who needed no interpreter, least of all one so little interested in the grand strategy of war as Mr. Mackenzie King, out-manoeuvred him by making their great decisions not with Canada but in Canada, allowing Mr. King to play host and little more at the two Quebec Conferences where allied policy was shaped. This unhappy and inaccurate definition of Canada's role is part of the assumption that Canada is a country whose culture, government, speech, and habits of life can always be identified as something half British or French and half American, a handy formula for foreigners but of dubious validity. For Canadians this concept of themselves as a eunuch nation with no purpose of their own has stood in the way of self-confident national development and the exploitation of the Canadian vocation.

For most of its history Canada was not a linchpin but a hostage; a common reluctance to get involved in war in or over Canada was a powerful inducement for the United States and Britain to get along peacefully. Perhaps the historian Churchill saw Canada as the linchpin, however, because he realized that when Canada was committed in 1939 to the war against Hitler, the United States, having promised through the words of Roosevelt in 1938 not to stand idly by if domination of Canadian soil was threatened, was in the long run committed also, like a wheel to a carriage. Canada in the past has been a territory which complicated relations between Britain and the United States and perhaps inevitably involved them in each other's struggles. This historic role has little relevance, however, to the present situation. One of the strongest elements in the link between Canada and Britain under present circumstances is that they are common allies of and both dependent on the United States. If any of the three were attacked, it is virtually certain that the other two would come to its defence, but this act would take place within a framework of alliance and international organization that robs the role of Canada of particular significance as a link.

The triangle figure, however, does have validity. An authoritative spokesman, Paul Nitze, recently defined the position of the United States vis-à-vis its associates as follows: "A pattern of political relationships . . . characterized by exceptionally close collaboration between the United States, England, and Canada, spreading out through close, but not so close, relationships with Germany, France, Italy, and Japan, and shading off to cooperation on certain basic matters with the uncommitted but free countries such as India and Burma." (This was written before Mr. Nitze became an official of the United States Defense establishment.)

It has become currently fashionable to deny the existence of any special relationship among "les Anglo-Saxons." Such a relationship cannot be officially acknowledged or specifically institutionalized, of course, but in practice there is, as General de Gaulle knows full well, a unique element of commitment, priority, and candour in the relations of the United States, Britain, and Canada, an element rooted in habit and history, a fact of life not a contract. Within this eternal triangle, however, Canada is not the intercessor but the junior of two junior partners. It should be noted, furthermore, that the Canadian role is regional; on Far Eastern questions Australia rather than Canada would enjoy this intimacy.

Canada as interpreter

Even though it has been exaggerated, there remains some validity in the concept of Canada as interpreter. On a personal rather than a national level, Canadians play a part in justifying Britons and Americans to each other. In the Suez Crisis of 1956, Canada perhaps came closest to the classical role. Although both Canada and the United States disagreed with British and French policy at that time, there was considerable difference in their postures. The official American demeanour was one of cold anger, and at the United Nations involved a virtual severance of personal relations, but there was much more of sorrow than of anger in the Canadian position. Contacts of the frankest, and in their own way sympathetic, kind were maintained throughout between British and Canadian leaders, and with Indians and Pakistanis as well. As the Americans and British in a critical situation were barely speaking to each other, the Canadian Minister of External Affairs, Mr. Pearson, and his associates had furiously to interpret. Canada maintained a middle position in the dispute because, although the Canadian Government had been appalled at British and French actions, it became appalled also by the petulant and rudderless policy of the United States as the crisis wore on. Much has been written about the reasons which led Britain to withdraw from Egypt, and they were undoubtedly varied. Nevertheless, Canadian persuasion, not because it reflected the view of one small country but because it reflected the views of most of the Commonwealth, the United States, a majority in the United Nations, and, by no means of least importance, a great deal of influential opinion in Britain, played a not inconsiderable part.

It might be noted here that a lesser power can sometimes usefully represent in international diplomacy views held by a minority in one of the great powers. Sometimes Canadian positions have served to reflect minority or unofficial opinion in the United States. One of the functions of Canada may be to precipitate into international discussion points of view held by many Americans but not accepted by the Administration for export. This could be particularly useful on China policy, for example, on which there has been until recently less free discussion within the United States than is customary in the American tradition. It goes without saying, of course, that it is tactically unwise ever to align a government directly with the views of the Opposition in a large friendly power.

Insofar as Canada acted as interpreter to the United States since the last war, the role was that of interpreter not of the British ally but of the nonaligned within the Commonwealth. Canada accepted with enthusiasm the new perspectives of the Commonwealth after India and Pakistan joined in 1947. Canada used its influence to see that the Commonwealth's evolution as a multiracial organization was not frustrated by nostalgic imperialism. Having itself recently embarked on a broader field of international policy, Canada found in the Commonwealth association with new Asian, and later African, states a source of perspective on world politics and an asset in diplomacy. Having experienced the transition from dependent status to independence and the frustrations of limited power, Canadians were able to comprehend with sympathy the neuroses of independence and the instinct to neutralism in these new nations. Although rejecting neutralism for themselves, Canadians accepted sooner than Americans the wisdom of nonalignment for weak countries. This difference of approach was particularly marked during the Dulles regime when there was often something approaching a consensus among Commonwealth members about the Asian questions which preoccupied the world at that time. This consensus separated them as a group from the more rigid attitudes of Washington. Canada's influence on Washington, such as it was, was less effective in direct pleading than through playing an active role in the United Nations and in behind-the-scenes diplomacy along with the Indians and others to prevent a confrontation over the Korean settlement, American prisoners in China, the Indo-China truces, or the offshore islands. In the State Department he was known sometimes as "Swami Pearson," but the Canadian Secretary of State for External Affairs and the Prime Minister, Mr. St. Laurent, as well, exerted themselves not only to explain Nehru to Dulles but to convince Delhi and, through Delhi, Peking of the intentions of the United States. It was fortunate that these differences between the United States and Canada in the Far East and in the United Nations occurred at a time when Canada was playing such an enthusiastic role in the development of NATO that Canadian heresy on Eastern issues was looked upon in Washington as aberration rather than perfidy.

These were of course phenomena of a certain period; the pattern lingers because it was the period of the flowering of Canadian diplomacy. It was not required that Canada pose as an interpreter between India and Washington in 1964, just as it was less necessary then for Canada to argue the case for nonalignment. The role of interpreter is dependent on the juxtaposition of personalities and policies. The change of government in the United States in 1961 and in Canada in 1963 gave the two countries leadership by men with a basically similar *Weltanschauung*. Such a situation made for more harmonious relations, although it perhaps also reduced the significance of the Canadian role in the world as interpreter. Fluctuations in both the international and national scene can, of course, reverse these trends at any time.

There is one thing permanent in the Canadian qualification for the role of interpreter—its minor status. Lesser powers do achieve among themselves an ease of conversation that is inevitably more difficult between those who are disparate in size. This is by no means automatic. Certain smaller European powers, by reason of an imperial past or cultural arrogance, have been singularly unsuccessful in their dealing with new countries, much less successful in fact than the all-powerful United States. Having lacked the same opportunities to practise imperialism and racial discrimination, Canadians have some advantage over the Europeans and even over the United States in dealing with the newly independent states at a time when most of the issues which flare in the world are concerned with race and colonialism. The role of an honest broker is, of course, peripheral rather than decisive. It is the weight of the great power, as provider of economic assistance and protection or as the avenging fury, which finally determines whether or not a settlement or compromise will be reached. Nevertheless, the interpreter's minor role is essential and complementary, sometimes the *sine qua non*. It does not follow that the Canadian, because he is a Canadian, is accepted as a trusted counsellor by the developing peoples. However, if he is disposed, as most Canadians tend to be, to comprehend the attitudes of newly independent peoples, he finds the incapacity of his country to threaten and command a considerable asset.

A bridge to France?

A word of caution needs to be said on another notion about Canada's role, because of its bicultural nature, as a link between the French and the Anglo-Saxons. This is a role well worth striving after, as it is badly needed in the present state of Atlantic tensions, but it should be approached without illusions about the realities of recent relations between France and Canada. French Canada is also French America, a harmonization of elements which might be significant. In its attitudes to the world, however, French-Canadian nationalism finds the foreign policies of neither Washington nor Paris congenial. Growing antagonism to the Anglo-Saxons who dominate the continent has inspired a new stirring of the French blood, but there has in the past been little pressure from French Canada to align Canadian foreign policy with that of France. There are probably no two NATO capitals, in fact, between which there has been so little sympathy as Ottawa and Paris. Their views on colonial issues, on world order, on the United Nations, and on the role of lesser powers in world affairs have been opposed for a decade at least. The French have not concealed their disdain for the upstart diplomatic pretensions of Canada, and their xenophobia has made little exception for the gallant people who have kept French culture alive in America for centuries. The revival of the French spirit in Canada has coincided with Gaullist nationalism in France. André Malraux, with a message of cultural fraternity, has been warmly received in Quebec, and Prime Minister Pearson has made a visit to Paris with the clear intention, both for national and international reasons, of strengthening Canadian-French relations. These relations might well become more cordial, but the stubborn differences in world perspectives remain.

The attitude of French Canada in the relationship

One of the partial truths repeated about the United States and Canada is that they share a common language and political philosophy. Canada is, however, a country with two official languages. One third of the Canadians, who speak French, look out on the world with a viewpoint unlike that of English Canada and still more unlike that of the United States. Canadian foreign policy is the product of governments in which English and French-speaking Canadians take part. There is not an English-Canadian foreign policy contending with a French-Canadian foreign policy, but there are variations in emphasis. Heretofore the English-Canadian emphasis has undoubtedly predominated, but it may be tempered to a greater extent in future by the French-Canadian emphasis. French Canada has of late been moved by a powerful political-cultural revolution and is asserting not only the rights of its language but of its political philosophy. As a result Canadian foreign policy could be paralyzed by domestic difference or it might be adjusted towards the Quebec view in ways which would widen the gap between American and Canadian foreign policies. It should not be assumed that differences between English and French-Canadians on this subject are based on ties with their respective motherlands. Both have been largely weaned. The renaissance of the French spirit led by Charles de Gaulle has given cultural inspiration to Quebec, but there is nothing of political *enosis* in Quebec's attitude to France. French-Canadians are more American continentalists than are English-Canadians, less tied to Europe, anti-colonialist by tradition, suspicious of a Mother Country which long ago lost interest in them, and inspired by the nationalist movements in North Africa and Latin America. They are not so much hostile to the United States as out of sympathy with it, not opposed to NATO but anti-militarist, anxious to keep Canada out of the nuclear business, sympathetic with Latins and others who resist the domination of the great English-speaking power, anti-communist but with some fellow-feeling for Castro. They accuse English-Canadians of being too subservient to American foreign policy and too little nationalist. So important is it for Canada to find common ground between French and English Canada that more attention will probably be paid by the government to these attitudes. Drastic changes are unlikely. French-Canadians in the mass do not differ from English-Canadians, or from Americans, in their fundamental attitudes to peace, freedom, and the threat of totalitarianism. Nevertheless, their increasing influence in Canadian policy is likely to strengthen rather than weaken the Canadian disposition to preserve its diplomatic independence, resist too close military and political involvement with the United States, and emphasize Canada's association with the Latin and French-speaking world as well as with the Anglo-Saxons. It is not an easily predictable factor but one which should be borne in mind in looking to the future.

The Relationship and the World Economy

This essay is concerned primarily with international political rather than economic relations, but the United States-Canadian relationship is, of course, deeply enmeshed in the world economy. Here as elsewhere in international relations the political and the economic cannot be disentangled, but in economic questions the Alliance is of less significance. The Cold War is a minor factor, and the United States and Canada are as likely to be antagonists as collaborators in international economic diplomacy. On a question such as the sale of wheat, which blew up a storm between the two countries in the autumn of 1963, the United States viewed Canada as its principal antagonist and accused Ottawa of disregarding established rules of consultation on wheat prices. The Canadian view was that obligation to consult which applies in matters of Western security could hardly apply when one is trying to beat a competitor. In other major economic issues of recent years, as for example the question of Britain and the European Economic Community, there was no very substantial meeting of minds between Ottawa and Washington because the two capitals saw their own interests as different. Discussion did, of course, continue among down-the-line officials in spite of strain at the top, because on all major international issues it has become ritualistic. Such disputes are, in a sense, taken for granted by two peoples who believe in the sacred principle of competition. Charges may be hurled across the border over the price of wheat to Japan, but both sides recognize that business is business. Each side may complain shrilly that the other side in its commercial practice is not behaving like an ally defending the free world, but it is doubtful if he takes his own debating point too seriously.

To trade or not to trade with communists?

It is when international political considerations become involved in trade policy that there can be bitterness. The root of much present trouble is that the two countries have different attitudes on trade as an instrument of political policy. Canada, which is much more dependent on trade than is the United States, is much more reluctant to interrupt commerce for political reasons. Both subscribe to the NATO rules restricting the export of strategic materials to communist countries. Canada, however, has displayed less confidence in the efficacy of embargoes and has leaned usually towards liberalizing the rules. It has treated all communist countries alike; in particular it has not differentiated between China and the Soviet Union, whereas the United States has reserved its special discrimination for Asian communist states. The enormous sales of wheat which Canada made in late 1963, not only to China but also to the Soviet Union and other Eastern European countries, gave a substantial lift to the health of the Canadian economy. Sales of wheat to China by the Conservative government were credited with maintaining for the Conservatives the prairie vote in the elections of 1962 and 1963. Although duly sceptical about the long-range future of the communist market, it has become a factor which no Canadian government can take lightly—infinitely more important to the Canadian economy than to the American. When Mr. Paul Martin argued, during the NATO Council meeting in Paris in November 1963, on behalf of increased trade with the East on the grounds that "isolation of the communist world is not in the interest of the détente as it is now developing," he might be accused of having had his eye on more immediate and material aims. However, the argument was consistent with the views and policies of Canadian governments for many years, even when sales to that area seemed improbable.

Canada has not recognized the Peking regime, but it has dealt informally with its agents and allowed Canadians to visit China and Chinese to come to Canada. As for Cuba, which is not formally included by Ottawa in the Soviet bloc, Canada, like most other NATO countries, acted on the principle that diplomatic and economic isolation of the Castro regime would serve only to drive it into the arms of the Eastern Europeans and Chinese. Although Canadian trade with Cuba had never been significant, exports to that country rose for a brief period when the Cubans were looking for substitutes for American imports and then dwindled as Cubans ran out of foreign exchange. These matters of commerce, however, touched political issues on which Americans felt deeply, and they have caused more ill will between the two countries than most issues of world politics. In American eyes it may be excusable for Canadians to play the normal game of commercial advantage but not when it looks like aiding the enemies of the United States and taking advantage of American self-denial. In the Canadian view, however, these embargoes are unwise and unilateral. Canadians have been less inclined than Americans to see the overthrow of communist regimes as a feasible aim and have been more disposed, therefore, to hope that the beneficent influence of commerce would eventually erode barriers and create on both sides vested interests in peaceful relations. The argument on principle is apt to sound naïve, and Canadians more frequently argue pragmatically that economic discrimination for political reasons against the Soviet Union, China, and Cuba has never proved its efficacy as an instrument of policy in practice.

A source of popular irritation in Canada has been the export policies of American subsidiaries in Canada. There is first the Canadian fear that the United States parents, for reasons of company policy, will not permit their Canadian subsidiaries to export at all. The more disturbing fear, however, is that they will attempt to apply regulations inspired by United States foreign policy to the operation of Canadian companies, raising thereby the question of extra-territorial sovereignty. Importance was attached to two well-publicized occasions on which orders from Communist China to two Canadian subsidiaries of American automobile industries were said to have been refused because of instructions from Detroit. The cases were, however, less conclusive than they seemed. The Chinese orders were themselves vague and the United States Secretary of State, after conversations with Canadian leaders and anxious to prevent friction, made specific provision that American regulations could be waived on request to permit orders of this kind to be filled.

Canada has, of course, a special problem over American embargoes because of its long border. Even when, as in the case of Cuba, it does not join in the embargo, it must prevent its soil from becoming an entrepôt through which American goods can be bootlegged to the embargoed country. Cooperation with the United States in these cases is not only a matter of neighbourly assistance but also a recognition that the United States must not be tempted to impose restrictions against contraband trade across the vast Canadian border which could play havoc with normal trade. The interrelation of the two economies is such that although Canada can and does pursue distinct political-economic policies, it can never ignore the interests and sensitivities of the large neighbour.

The impression should not be left that, whereas the two countries are allies in politics, they are antagonists in economics. The economic causes which unite them are deeper than those which divide even though they attract less constant attention. The political and military reasons for the Alliance may not require a common policy on economic questions, but they do curb the spirit of unlimited competition. Overriding mutual interest in the health of the "free world," freedom of trade, and the peaceful development of poor countries not only restrains Canada and the United States from throat-cutting but also draws them together in such broad causes as freeing the channels of world trade. After some hesitation and a change of government, Canada offered moral support for President Kennedy's Trade Expansion Program. This moral support did not, however, align Canada in support of the United States in the Geneva negotiations, because the Canadian government thought that the bases of American negotiation needed modification if Canada was not to be damaged in the process. When their interests do coincide, however, as in their approach to the EEC over its common agricultural policy, the two keep closely in step.

In trade negotiations Canada is likely to find itself in a stronger position than in political or strategic negotiations because Canada is more of a power in the world economy than it is in world strategy. On a per-capita basis, it is one of the world's largest trading nations, but its significance for other countries is best indicated by the fact that in volume Canada imports from the world at large one third as much as does the United States with ten times the population. The effect on the American farmer of Canada's huge wheat sale in the autumn of 1963 was so great that the United States, began seriously to consider altering its whole policy on trade with communists. It is difficult to imagine any political or defence issue on which the effect of Canadian action could be so important.

On economic questions the uniqueness of the continental relation is more significant. The economies are so closely linked that Canada does require, and usually gets, special treatment because American legislation designed to cope nationally with foreign countries in general could prove disastrous to Canada. Because of the enormous United States investment in Canada, if for no other reason, such a result would not be in American interests. That is why Canada, for instance, has been given special treatment on oil-production sharing and equalization tax exemption.

Canadian and American Perspectives on the World

There are variations in the world perspective of great and middle-sized powers even when their interests, their education, and their philosophies are close. For one thing the great power is bound to have a stronger sense of responsibility and therefore to be more conservative in its approach. It does not follow that the lesser power is condemned to irresponsibility, for its freedom from responsibility can be useful. A country like Canada can espouse a new approach to disarmament or display, for example, a positive interest, as it did, in exploring Mr. Rapacki's plans for disengagement in Europe. The United States must be more cautious because its position is decisive. Trial balloons must be floated, ideas explored without commitment, and discussions held with antagonists. This is a useful function for the middle power, although it must be careful to give no false impression of its mandate. It is a function which Poland, for instance, can fulfill on the other side, and for this reason Canadian-Polish explorations have on occasion been to some purpose. A mutual acceptance of the value of this role is desirable because irritation is aroused by the impatience of Americans with Canadians for putting up unacceptable ideas whereas Canadians underestimate the caution with which the United States must move from an established position. That far-out ideas are not always fanciful or feckless may be illustrated by the fact that one idea Canadian leaders first put up for public discussion in 1948 was the creation of a North Atlantic Treaty Organization.

There are between the United States and Canada differences of perspective which are the product of quite different histories. History is responsible for Canada's being more Atlantic-minded and less Pacific or Western Hemisphere-oriented. Canada had no violent break with Europe and grew up feeling that Britain, and somewhat more remotely France, were part of its own flesh. Not being Pacific-minded, Canada left the Pacific War almost entirely to the United States and the present defence of the area to SEATO and other security arrangements—to none of which Canada is a party. It is inevitable that Canada should feel less a partner of the United States in the East than in the West. Canada has its own interests on the far side of the Pacific, but, aside from important links with its third most important trading partner, Japan, these ties have developed through the Commonwealth with India, Pakistan, Ceylon, and, of course, Australia and New Zealand. Canadian troops served in Korea and they are in the truce commissions in Indo-China, but these obligations have been accepted rather as responsibilities to the international community than to the American ally.

Hemisphere perspectives

The different world perspectives of the two countries are illustrated also in their view of where they are geographically. The United States, however widespread its operations, has thought of itself as belonging to the Western Hemisphere; Canada has seen itself primarily as a country of the Northern Hemisphere. The Western Hemisphere as the United States and Latin America see it is more a historical than a geographical phenomenon, based on revolutionary and republican traditions which Canada has not shared. Canada's ties were with Europe; the historical threat to its security came not from overseas but from the south, and its concepts of security were more imperial than continental. All this has changed radically, although with some cultural lag. Now, however, when Canadians are disposed to recognize their common security interest with the United States and the increasing importance of the southern part of the Western Hemisphere to their safety, they have become so deeply involved in the wide world that many of them are sceptical of the validity of this kind of regionalism. What is more important, they have got themselves so busy and so committed in other continents that they are cautious about the consequences of involvement in inter-American activities.

There is, nevertheless, a good deal of support among Canadians for affiliation with the Organization of American States, and statements by both the present Liberal Secretary of State for External Affairs and his Conservative predecessor indicate their belief that this is a course which deserves serious consideration. Support comes from those who believe that Latin America is a region of crisis and that Canada, by reason in particular of its mediatory experience, has an obligation to throw itself into the politics and economics of the area; from those also who have been bewitched by American rhetoric into attaching a mystical significance to the Isthmus of Panama and assuming that somehow or other Paraguayans have more right to Canadian concern than Nigerians; and also from French-Canadians who think of themselves as part of "Latin America" and seek allies against the Anglo-Saxon domination of North America. Majority opinion may move to support this move, but Canada is unlikely to consider a Pan American alignment as being exclusive and incompatible with such traditional associations as the Commonwealth. Indications, however, that Latin American countries have been reluctant to accept such an ambivalent position for the sister Commonwealth nations of Jamaica and Trinidad have given Ottawa cause—and an excuse—to pause. As for the diplomatic consequences of membership in a "Hemisphere club," Canadian opinion is divided along typical lines. There are those who think Canada should seek a new mission as catalytic agent in the neurotic relations between Latin America and the United States, and those who cannily fear that Canada has enough international political reasons for differing with its great neighbour and should not add an enormous area of complication. The United States, after opposing Canadian membership up to World War II out of fear that Canada would be a British agent in the pure republican air of Pan America, has come round to supporting as tactfully as possible Canadian entry. This attitude does the United States credit, for it must realize that Canada would not be a complaisant associate and might well join heretics like Mexico and Brazil over Cuban issues. On the other hand, the United States would like Canadian help, both diplomatic and material, and is far-sighted enough to recognize that although Canada could be tactically troublesome, the two countries would be working towards the same ultimate goals.

Remnants of isolation

Until 1941 Canada's record was less isolationist than that of the United States, although its attitude was always that of a country more passively than actively drawn into world affairs. The imperial tie was strong enough for Canadians during the past century to be involved in fighting both in Africa and Europe while the United States remained aloof, but the involvement was always at second hand through Britain. Since World War II both nations have cast off isolationism and dedicated themselves to the maintenance of world order everywhere. Isolationist instincts persist in both countries in different forms. Whereas some Americans want to reject the awful burden of responsibility thrust upon them, some Canadians would contract out of responsibility by, as a small power, leaving things to those who may be disposed to run the world.

The policy of the smaller state, however, is bound to look more isolationist than that of a nuclear power. Because its resources are limited by its size, even if they were more generously deployed, Canada's active participation in world affairs must be more selective than that of the United States. For example, Canada confines its economic aid largely to Commonwealth and French-speaking dependent countries, whereas the United States, to which all countries turn, finds infinitely greater political difficulties involved in being selective. The fact that Canadian aid is rarely on such a scale as to determine the survival of the recipient means also that Canada is less troubled than the United States by the problem of whether or not the aid has "strings." Canada can confine its military effort to the defence of North America and Western Europe and to international peace-keeping operations, leaving the Pacific and South Atlantic to the United States and others. Tactically and economically this makes good sense. There is no justification for parcelling out Canadian aid or forces in ineffective driblets.

Temperamental variations

It has often been suggested that there are temperamental differences between Americans and Canadians in their world views because of their different histories. Here one must tread warily. These conclusions are usually posited on the apparent fact that Canadians tend to see the world in grays while Americans see things in black and white, but the latter is an attitude which hardly characterizes the supple foreign policy inaugurated by President Kennedy. One reason, of course, for a more relaxed perspective by Canadians on the Cold War is that their feelings are not incited daily by irrational attacks on them. Canada has been largely ignored by communist spokesmen, including Castro, except as a vehicle through which to attack the United States. Although Canadians resent the attacks on their friends, the sting is not the same. The disposition by Canadians to compromise is often attributed to their history; to a less absolutist attitude towards the state; to the patience that comes of an evolutionary rather than a revolutionary tradition; and to the fact that as citizens of a state in which two nations live, Canadians are used to accepting peaceful coexistence, of living with intractable facts and turning them into advantages rather than trying to remove them by force. Canada has not only avoided revolution, it has never sought to settle its domestic dissensions by civil war. Politically the Canadian is a different animal from the American, however similar his cultural pattern, and it is inevitable that his internal political attitudes affect his external attitudes. In a turbulent and dangerous world in which war must be avoided at almost any cost, there is much to be said for the Canadian disposition to find situations tractable, provided that it is not carried too far in tiresome insistence that the powers negotiate when there is no room for negotiation. If one sees these American and Canadian instincts towards intransigence and appeasement not as ultimate principles but in terms of checks and balances, one can find strength in the interplay.

Canada in the American world perspective

For Canadians relations with the United States in foreign policy are a constant preoccupation—too much so; for Canada's international role would be more effective if Canadians could see themselves less as the neglected and overshadowed neighbour and more as an upper-middle-class performer moving on terms of equality with many other nations of the world. For the United States, on the other hand, Canada is far from being a subject of preoccupation, although it is often viewed as a problem, *sui generis.* American policy makers do not deny its importance, situated as it is, but they are too busy round the world to pay much attention to a country which can be tiresome but is unlikely to be dangerous. Charles Burton Marshall recognizes that, "A sundering of a constitution and the imposition of military despotism in Pakistan concerns us, to be sure, but a like occurrence in Canada would concern us vastly more." This is true, but the fact is that Canada is too habitually stable to attract this concern. Canada's place in the American scheme of things is hard to define. The United States is bound to consult the interests of all its allies, to receive their ambassadors in times of crisis, pay official visits to their capitals, and call them all "free and equal partners." It must not, however, classify or even seem to classify these associates in order of priority. That Britain is still *primus inter pares* can hardly be doubted. The priority of others, Germany or France, Brazil or the Philippines, depends on the issue at stake. The positions of Mexico and Canada are unique, Canada claiming special intimacy because of the long frontier, at least one common language, and the military alliance. Canada is *propinquimus* rather than *primus,* a factor which might induce a new American President to pay his first foreign trip to Ottawa but does not automatically put the Canadian Ambassador at the head of the queue at the State Department.

Friends but also foreigners

A Canadian ambassador once chided informally the American Secretary of State because the Canadian Governor-General had been received with casual protocol, whereas for the President of Mexico's visit to Washington the school children were given a holiday and the streets draped. The Secretary of State indicated surprise that Canadians would want to be treated thus like foreigners. One of the difficulties of the relationship arises from the reluctance on both sides to call each other foreigners—an attitude which reveals less about the fraternal relations between them than about their xenophobiac attitude to the word "foreigner." Canadians feel that Americans forget about Canada in their foreign relations because they think of it—benevolently, but inaccurately—as some kind of extension of their own country. The Canadian attitude is, however, ambivalent. Canadians are not flattered by being told they are "just like Americans," but on the other hand they would be unhappy if they thought they were being placed in the same category as countries that Americans and Canadians would both call "foreigners." Prime Minister Pearson suggested to a meeting of the Pilgrims in New York (November 6, 1963) that, "It would be wise for Americans to consider any Canadian Government as a friendly *foreign* one whose first responsibility is the protection of the national interests of its own people; which includes as a very important element . . . the necessity of close cooperation with a good and gigantic friend and neighbour."

The Atlantic perspective and "the dumbbell"

The apparent ignoring of Canada's existence was notable when American policy was dominated by the so-called dumbbell theory of Atlantic relations—that neat conception in which an already packaged United States was to be balanced by a newly packaged Europe (including the British and Irish islands) in a directorate of the "free world." That it was not a scheme which Canadians were likely to find attractive either escaped the attention of Washington or, probably, was not considered important. The dumbbell reigned at a time when the United States was especially exasperated with Canadian foreign policy and the element of not caring might have been as large as that of not knowing. It was not a deliberate American calculation to incorporate Canada in its end of the dumbbell because the United States was showing little appetite for such an indigestible morsel. The omission of consideration for one of the founder members of NATO might be excused on the ground that the Canadian military contribution to NATO, while reliable, was far from crucial. It was more surprising, however, that President Kennedy's Trade Expansion Act of 1962, which also reflected the preoccupation with Europe, was based on provisions which took into consideration only the United States and the enlarged European Common Market. Canada was not mentioned in the so-called "dominant supplier" section which provided for reduction or elimination of tariffs on commodities for which the United States and the EEC accounted for 80 per cent of "free world" exports. The enthusiasm of Washington for a potential market of some 250 millions is understandable, but the fact remained that United States trade with Canada was greater than that with all of the existing EEC and about two thirds that with the whole of Europe. The lack of attention to an important partner was attributable partly to the failure of the Canadian government to throw itself into constructive collaboration to meet the situation expected after Britain joined the Market, but the infatuation of Washington with its vision of a united Europe and the symmetry of the dumbbell suggested an unwillingness to think of Canada as a foreign affair at all. Since then, however, an adjusted appreciation of West European policy seems to have restored Washington to a less tidy view of the world—and one in which Canada can breathe more freely.

Traditionally the United States attitude to Canada in the Atlantic Community was more congenial than the dumbbell. Canada has been regarded as a junior partner whose presence in Atlantic councils completes the symmetry of the trans-oceanic relationship, gives reassurance of the North American commitment to Europe, and adds flexibility to the trans-Atlantic equation. This was the spirit of NATO and more recently of the transformation of the OEEC into the OECD, in which both the United States and Canada (and later Japan) joined with the European members. In NATO and OECD the United States could look upon Canada as a special partner from its own neighbourhood even though Canada, in NATO diplomacy, traditionally collaborated with the smaller European members, resisted proposals for a great power directorate, and failed to support many favourite American proposals such as the multilateral nuclear force. Canada (by its unique position as an independent middle-sized American power) has helped make NATO work. The Atlantic Community best finds its equilibrium in diversity. However plausible the argument for a united Europe on the one hand and some kind of united North America on the other, there are reasons historical, psychological, and diplomatic, why the checks and balances to be found in a community in which Britain, Ireland, the Scandinavian countries, and Canada are free-wheeling entities provide a more harmonious and a workable pattern than the dumbbell.

Expectations and Frustrations in Perspective

Canada is a great flank in United States defence. Washington needs to feel assured that Canada will, neither deliberately nor through neglect, allow its soil to be used by another power to breach American defences. On this subject there is no serious reason for the United States to fear. Through NORAD and NATO Canada has accepted its military responsibility as an ally to cooperate in the defence of United States power as the principal arm of the Western alliance. There is uneasiness in the United States, however, over what is looked upon as "neutralism" and "anti-Americanism" in Canada, and this uneasiness may be a factor in undermining the spirit of cooperation in world affairs. Canadian policy, however, has for many years been based on a shrewd realization that it must maintain its defences to the world if for no other reason than that it must never tempt the United States to move in for its own protection. The exaggeration of the force of "neutralism" and "anti-Americanism" may be attributable to a failure to discriminate between embedded hostility, as it exists in Latin America or Europe, and lively but *ad hoc* criticisms of American policies which flourish among a neighbouring people deeply involved in the consequences of United States foreign policy. Certain Canadian policies, vis-à-vis Cuba and China, for example, seen against this erroneous impression of Canadian "neutralism" take on a more sinister aspect than they warrant.

Mr. Paul Martin declared (August 24, 1963):

> We live in an inter-dependent world and ultimately our relations with the communist world are governed by the general state of East-West relations and particularly by the climate and the relations between the United States and the Soviet Union. Because of these facts it is neither possible nor desirable that our relations with the communist world should be at wide variance with those of our closest friends and allies. Yet within these limits there are possibilities open to us which serve our interests and the interests of our allies.

Both countries would pursue their policies more happily and more effectively if Americans would relax in the assurance that, however independent Canadian actions are in world politics, Canadian policy is governed by an almost universal recognition that Canada has no possibility and no intention of remaining neutral if the United States is involved in a major war. Furthermore, if the United States were involved in even limited military operations, against North Vietnam or Cuba for example, in which Canadian participation would neither be required nor forthcoming, the Canadian position would be at the very least that of a "friendly nonbelligerent." Americans should understand that Canada may go on differing in its relations with Cuba in the belief, even if this is not shared in Washington, that its policy does no harm to the interests of the Western Alliance, but if there should be another confrontation as in October 1962, it would declare its solidarity even if it were not in total agreement. Encouraging the United States to take ultimate Canadian support for granted does, of course, rob Canada of the chance to gain attention by acting coy and hard to please. In the long run, however, it is better for Canadians to suffer the frustration of being taken for granted than to risk the inevitable consequences of seduction.

As a troublemaker, therefore, Canada may be counted on to play the role within limits. A present cause of annoyance, however, has to do with the more positive American expectation of Canada, that it lend its weight to American causes. Canada is considered to have been dragging its feet on a number of fronts. The lack of clarity in its defence effort is the subject of some bitterness. It has been chided also for not doing its share in economic aid to developing countries. There is a belief that Canada has been neglecting its responsibility in what, according to American mythology, is "our Hemisphere." There is some feeling also that Canada is not acting boldly enough in the great crusade to reduce the barriers of trade, but the tendency to accuse each other of "economic nationalism" whenever one party's commercial interests seem to be affected puts this complaint in a special category. These alleged Canadian defaults might have been more acceptable in American eyes if Canada had of late been proving its usefulness more frequently by its middle-power role in the United Nations. Although the Canadian contribution to peace-keeping has never been widely acknowledged or appreciated among the American public, President Kennedy did once call it "an important and consecutive role." In recent years this role has been maintained but in situations where the Canadian function was less dramatically evident than over Suez or Indo-China.

In their expectations of Canada—or of any other ally for that matter—Americans would be wise to recognize that the Alliance is not the free and equal partnership we feel obliged to continue saying it is. The United States, as a consequence of history and its own genius, finds itself in the position of special responsibility for defending the "free world." It determines the crucial decisions not by an unreasonable assumption of authority but by its control over military resources and techniques. This is a fact of contemporary life, not a cause of complaint. However, it is equally a fact that those without responsibility for decisions cannot feel responsibility to share equally in the burdens. Smaller powers, having less voice, cannot be expected to carry a proportionate share either of military or economic obligations. There are many advantages, psychological as well as material, in being a great power, and great powers have always had to pay for these advantages with their cash and their blood. This is, of course, rougher talk than political leaders can indulge in, because the principle of an alliance in which all must share the burdens and decisions must be maintained as a public posture. However, it is advisable to recognize as a working principle that there is an inevitable relationship between contribution and policy-making (just as there was a connexion between taxation and representation). Canada does not and is unlikely in foreseeable circumstances to contribute to Western defence in amounts proportionate to the United States. If Americans are irritated by this disparity, they must not forget the disparity in decision-making. Canadians, on the other hand, should realize that if they assume tacitly that they are not obliged to equal burden-sharing with the Americans, their grounds are weaker for resenting the American assumption of a right to a decisive influence on policy.

Canadian initiatives under the Conservative regime, particularly in disarmament, were not at all well regarded by Washington. The return to power of Mr. Pearson in the spring of 1963 revived regard for Canadian foreign policy and expectation of the fruits of both Canadian collaboration and of independent Canadian diplomacy in the general interest. A greater sense of partnership in world affairs was indicated at the Hyannis Port meeting of Mr. Pearson with President Kennedy shortly after he took office. These expectations, of course, tend to create illusions of total agreement which are bound to be dissipated and cause special bitterness. Since Mr. Pearson was last in action, moreover, United States foreign policy has changed. It has become more sure, confident, flexible—and in its sophisticated treatment of the Cold War more congenial to Canadians. At the same time United States power has become more nearly absolute and a fully collaborative Alliance more difficult. While the world outlook in Washington is more liberal and tolerant, the new self-confidence and the new competence stimulate intolerance in practice. A greater willingness in principle to listen to allies is combined with an honest doubt whether those who operate from a sideways perspective and without benefit of nuclear responsibility or the resources of Harvard and the RAND Corporation are likely to have views worth listening to.

The fundamental problem of the Canada-United States alliance in world affairs is one of perspective. Whereas the United States looms large in Canadian calculations, Canada is bound to have minor importance in the calculations of Washington on foreign relations. The fact is easily acknowledged, but the implications hard to assess. Unless they can be better comprehended on both sides, however, relations are bound to be not hostile but cranky, and fruitful collaboration unlikely. On most international issues the two peoples and the two governments are in fundamental agreement. They agree on the need to remain strong against the Communist threat while seeking opportunities to remove the reasons for fighting each other. From time to time they may differ in their attitudes to Vietnam, on the role the United Nations might play in Berlin, whether or not to trade with the Communists or to give them diplomatic recognition. These latter must be recognized as tactical differences on which it is healthy rather than unhealthy to have some debate among allies, provided neither one compromises by his policy the vital interests of the other. It can be taken for granted, of course, that during any international debate on tactics, there will be editors and politicians on both sides who will insist that vital national interests are at stake and passions will be roused. This kind of row must be accepted as inevitable even while we endeavour to reduce the heat by increasing understanding of the nature of the relationship and its implications. There is no easy formula to reduce friction in our world policies. It will not be achieved by the escape mechanisms beloved by North Americans: the creation of joint committees and the empty rhetoric of good will which denies the existence of conflicting interests. What is required is a greater readiness to listen to each other's explanations before roaring to conclusions, more awareness on the American side and more tolerance on the Canadian side, qualities which are not easily achieved in a far too busy world. Some scepticism about the possibility of ever achieving this state of mutual grace is part of the prescription. Those in control of policy on both sides should recognize that there will always be sour patches in the relationship which must be taken for granted and not confused and aggravated by charges of anti-Americanism on the one hand and arrogance on the other.

We have bored the world too long with sermons about our unfortified frontier. In a nuclear age the unfortified frontier between a super-nuclear power and one which could not defend itself for five minutes is an irrelevant symbol. Nevertheless, there are lessons in the successful partnership of a great and a small ally which are relevant not just in a world struggling to build and maintain alliances but also in a world just beginning to grapple with the problem of the relations between large powers and small neighbours in the appealing but fearsome state of disarmament.

Jacob Viner 

5

The Outlook for the Relationship

An American View

Geography and "The Problem"

To Canada today its over-all relations with the United States, including, and even emphatically so, its economic relations, are a "problem" for which the possibility of remedial action urgently needs exploration. There exists here a real problem, namely, the acute dissatisfaction of Canada with its relations to the United States, economic or otherwise. Whether there is substantial justification for this dissatisfaction, however, is a moral issue, not a question of fact which can be objectively answered. I will try to confine myself, therefore, to seeking explanation of attitudes rather than moral appraisals of them. Prevalent sentiments always have roots in pre-existing facts and events. The most obvious aspects of existing Canadian-American relationships which have made Canadians unhappy about their general pattern have roots in certain distinctive features of Canadian geography, both because of the nature of

---

Jacob Viner *is professor emeritus of economics, Princeton University. Born and educated in Canada, Professor Viner has had a distinguished career as a scholar at Princeton, and prior to that, at the University of Chicago. For many years active in government service, his assignments have included those of Assistant to the Secretary of the Treasury and Consultant, U. S. Department of State. Professor Viner has published extensively on international trade and economic development.*

these features in themselves, and because the impacts of these features on the pattern of Canadian-American economic relations is in part responsible for the Canadian dissatisfaction with that pattern.

Associated in a complex network of interacting variables with the geographical factors I have in mind is the disproportionate size of the countries, but "size" in other than a physical geography sense. Canada, in fact, has more acreage than the United States. But in senses other than purely physical—for instance, relative economic importance, relative numbers of people, aggregate or per-capita wealth and income, political and strategic status in world politics—lesser "size"—has (both in its direct psychologial influence and in its influence on the outcome of economic bargaining and of economic diplomacy between the two countries) combined and interacted with the impacts of physical geography, to generate the prevailing Canadian attitudes and opinions toward economic, political, and even cultural relations with the United States. Of course, factors other than "geography" and "size" have also contributed to this result.

If this were a discussion of Canadian-American relations as they were before World War I, it would have been necessary to take systematically into account what Canadian scholars have labelled as the triangular aspect of Canada's external relations, since the special relations of Canada with Britain, historical, economic, political, sentimental, were then of at least comparable importance to those with the United States. Britain, of course, continues to be important for Canada in a variety of ways, but in the economic field at least that importance has on the whole shrunk greatly. For present purposes it does not seem urgent to take it into account, or to apply qualifications to major conclusions because of it.

It has been stated earlier, the special geographical characteristics of Canada's boundaries are most conspicuous. Canada has a national frontier in common with only one country, the United States. The exceptionally long frontier is for much of its range physically easier for Canadians to cross than to travel along. The nearest third country is 1,500 miles or more from the major Canadian centers of population, and the nearest third country important to Canada, historically, politically, economically, culturally, is nearly 2,500 miles away. The great bulk of the Canadian population lives within commuting distance of the Canadian-American boundary. No other country in the world is similarly situated. Eire, in relation to Britain, perhaps comes closest to it in a number of respects. Argentina and Chile have a comparable long common frontier. But both of these countries have other neighbors; their boundary, for almost all of its length, is constituted by the Andes, an olympian fence instead of an invitation to contact; and in neither country does its population live clustered close to the boundary.

Not only is the common frontier of Canada and the United States for most of its range not a natural fence, but for much of its range it is for both countries a major facility for water transportation and an important common source of hydroelectric power. The two countries have joint (or overlapping) claims to the great water resources of their boundary areas, for use for drainage, navigation, and power purposes even in territories not in close proximity to these waters. The fisheries of the two countries also share use of these waters. Canada regards its limitation to a single bedfellow with respect to boundaries as enforcing upon it an undue degree of intimacy with its neighbor. If Providence, or history, or Britain, or the United States, had dealt fairly and with a reasonable degree of generosity with Canada's boundary, Canadians think it would have been located further south, or would have bordered on more than one country. It may even be that some Canadians regret that their boundary with the United States is not a replica of the Andes.

Complementary economics

Along with climatic and resource differences and resemblances, the differences in ratios of population to resources make the two countries highly complementary (in the absence of artificial barriers to trade) in their commercial relations with each other. Each country profits from this natural complementarity, and to some extent rejoices in it. But each also to some extent endeavors to undermine it by devising artificial obstructions to its natural operation. This is more markedly true of Canada, especially with respect to the export of unprocessed materials when, for what are now fortuitous historical reasons, the American federal government is prohibited by the Constitution from hampering export trade by milder means than outright export prohibitions and when the individual states have no power to and no motive for restricting exports by any means.

The essentially complementary character of the two economies results also in their having only one major natural product in common of which they are rival exporters, namely wheat. If forest products are treated as a single commodity, Sweden, Norway, and Finland present a parallel instance. But for these countries forest products constitute so important an element in their national economies that the restriction of their rivalry in export trade to these products leaves them still in the status of being predominantly competitors of each other for aggregate export trade. Judging by the effect of the rivalry between Canada and the United States in disposing of surplus wheat in third countries in recent years on the tempers of both countries, it is fortunate for both that their rivalry as exporters does not extend over a wide range of important commodities, and unfortunate that they do not study and adopt the Scandinavian pattern (whatever it may be) of dealing with such commercial rivalry as does occur among themselves.

Disparities in trade

Geography, disproportionality in economic size of the two countries, and a miscellany of other subordinate factors, result in the United States' being more important for Canada both as an export market for goods and services and as a source of imports than all the rest of the world combined. Eire, vis-à-vis Britain, Mexico vis-à-vis the United States, alone present parallel cases, except perhaps for some communist countries which have emerged from the colonial status only very recently. For the United States, on the other hand, Canada is important but not dominant both as an export market and as a source of imports. If percentages of total American GNP are used as criteria, its trade with Canada would seem to be a minor factor in American economy, but these measuring rods of economic importance have a strongly minimizing bias. To some Canadians it is a grievance that the United States looms so large in Canadian foreign trade, and a grievance also that United States trade with Canada does not loom larger in the American trade picture: not quite as self-contradictory a set of attitudes as it may seem at first glance, since each attitude is largely a logical byproduct of the Canadian resentment against the disproportionality of economic size of the two countries.

Another characteristic of present-day Canadian-American trade relationships is Canada's chronic excess of commodity imports from the United States over its commodity exports to the United States. It takes more than geographical factors and disproportionality of economic size to explain this result, but whatever the full explanation Canada does not like it; the United States presumably does. The respective disliking and liking can in turn, I think, be most easily explained as due to a survival in both countries of strong elements of mercantilist thought, especially in its more primitive form of rejoicing in "favorable" balances of trade and mourning over "unfavorable" balances of trade with *particular* countries, as distinguished from general or aggregate balances.

The Canadian Indictment

The interested but casual observer of trends of thought in Canada with respect to things American cannot escape the impression that a sense of grievance with the character and the mode of operation of the Canadian-American relationship is widespread in Canada, from taxi-drivers to journalists to finance ministers to prime ministers. Not unhappily, I have not encountered any instance of such bias on the part of Canadian economists, and I have found several Canadian economists who comment with some levity on the process of identifying, assembling, and counting grievances, one by one or in assorted packages. Were Canada as much dominated by American cultural patterns as some Canadians assert, I would regard these economists as running the risk of being charged with being fellow-travellers of the Americans.

Can old grievances be forgot?

The grievances are diverse, but they so interlock that almost all of them rest on actual or supposed facts economic in nature, or lead to calls for remedial action of a type which would have important economic consequences, or are natural psychological reactions, conscious or unconscious, to economic conditions which disturb national pride. Memories of the War of 1812, of the United States termination of trade reciprocity with Canada in the 1860's, of the Fenian Raids, of the successful conspiracies of Americans and British to move the Canadian frontiers northward and away from the seacoast, and so on, may be so live in Canada as to influence public opinion significantly. If so, however, I must presume that since the time, now long ago, when I knew something of Canadian education at first hand the teaching of Canadian history in Canada must have undergone a stupendous increase in quantity and effectiveness. That this has occurred is not hard to believe, nor that a detailed knowledge by Canadians of the history of the relations of Canada with the United States in the days of Manifest Destiny would not be likely of itself to arouse in them any deep sentiments of brotherly love. But I know of no pattern of educational effort which has caused more mischief since the emergence of nation-states than the systematic brooding within one state over ancient and irremediable grievances against another. For politicians it is sometimes a convenient substitute for struggling with internal grievances which may not be ancient but are refractory, but the educators should leave this political activity to the politicians, who, we may presume (or hope) would soon find it too repulsive or ineffective to be engaged in persistently and zealously. One should not, however, accept too sweepingly the irremediability of grievances merely because they are ancient. Those that cannot be forgotten, including those whose significance is confined to the fact that they survive as bitter memories, should be studied singly, and as unemotionally as possible, on the chance that there are still possibilities of obtaining by low-temperature persuasion and diplomacy some measure of symbolic reparation.

I have already argued that some of the Canadian grievances are really grievances against geography. Even where the geography is in a sense manmade, as when national boundaries were fixed or altered by the exercise of national power over a weaker neighbor, it is usually good statesmanship to treat it as irrevocable in the visible future. But the economic significance of a given geographical situation can be susceptible in some degree to contrived change, and technological progress, demographic developments, changes in tastes, and changes in trade policies of other countries may render a given geographical situation more favorable. Irrigation may turn a useless desert into a garden of plenty, or it may be discovered that untold mineral riches underlie it. Bush, muskeg, minerals, rushing waters, which have hitherto been useless or even nuisances can, with changes of technology or tastes or with the exhaustion of superior resources elsewhere, become valuable national resources. Growth of population at home may convert low-price export products into high-price deficit or import products, thus turning a problem conducive to international friction into a purely domestic one. Similarly, the exhaustion of a particular fishing-ground, while itself an economically costly change, may prevent international friction. All kinds of grievances, even geographical ones, may have been valid at some time in the past as grievances against Providence, or against a neighbor, but their significance except as unpleasant memories may soon largely or wholly evaporate.

Although the same processes of change which deprive some old grievances of real present-day significance can be safely counted on to accentuate the practical significance of other old grievances and to produce a crop of new ones, all I intend to suggest is the judicious selection of the grievances to brood over, to press, or to try gainfully to exploit.

Cultural protectionism

One of the factors that makes Canada a fertile field for grievances is the dissatisfaction of Canadians with the existing state (as they see it) of the Canadian national "identity," "unity," "cultural autonomy," "image." It has been common practice for countries, and for regions, which find themselves in such state to seek abroad instead of within themselves for the causes, and to lay the blame on their neighbor. As I have emphasized, Canada has only one neighbor. Trade is a great transmitter of culture, and the transmission of American "culture" abroad, by export of books, journals, the radio, television, the stage, songs and music, and via the open door to foreign tourists and students, has for the United States become in recent years a great trade. There is thus for Canada a considerable inducement to combine economic protectionism and cultural protectionism. On a recent visit to Canada I was surprised to find the customs officer uninterested in the contents of my luggage but very much interested in whether I was a carrier of architectural plans. The next stage might well be jamming the sound waves of American radio and television, a procedure I would tend to approve if such jamming were applied with discrimination, not merely on the basis of country of origin.

I do not present the behavior of the United States in this area as a model for any country to follow. We impose barriers to the entry of cultural material originating in communist countries. Without benefit of a Cold War alibi, we ration the entry of foreign actors. At least in the not-distant past, we have refused entry to foreign books which did not meet the nationally-discriminatory requirements of American Copyright Law, and have endeavored to impose on scholarly books eligible for entry *ad valorem* duties based not on the prices of the book but on their imputed cost of production to the publishers plus the cost of the research, scientific, archaeological, and so forth, behind the books. Since the American objectives were presumably wholly those of economic protectionism—and economic protectionism is universally culturally respectable, while cultural protectionism, the Cold War apart, is almost never respectable unless based on quality—even these American examples do not constitute much of a precedent for Canada.

Trade protectionism

American tariff policy is to Canadians a perennial grievance—as it also is to me, as the result, I have been frequently told, of a congenital ideological obsession. But Canadian tariff policy also has been to me a grievance. This no doubt disqualifies me as an objective appraiser of the two tariff barriers. The superior height of a particular country's tariff, in general, or in its particular impact on another country's trade, is usually regarded by that other country as a valid grievance, although it is rarely willing to apply the same principle to its own tariff in relation to the tariff of a third country which has, or seems to have, a still lower tariff. Here also I am confessedly disqualified as an objective commentator, since I not only am disinclined to judge the fruits of sin by the comparative sizes of the babies that result, but I am ignorant of any formula for reliable measurement of the comparative "height," in some significant sense, of any two tariffs in their most common forms, and regard as largely arbitrary all the formulae ordinarily used.

The question of equal treatment

Most countries long accepted as a minimum criterion of consistency of a country's tariff with international comity that it tax imports without regard to their country of origin (with trade between mother countries and their colonies usually expressly exempted from the rule), the so-called (unconditional) most-favored-nation rule. Until 1923, the United States rejected this rule in principle, but usually followed it in practice and often demanded adherence to it from other countries. (Exceptions are the decade of reciprocity with Canada and the preferential treatment given to Hawaii when quasi-independent and to Cuba.) Until the 1930's, Canada did not accept the rule, and from the 1890's to 1934 it withheld, to a limited extent, unconditional most-favored-nation treatment from the United States. As far as I know, the United States has never applied to any commodity imported from Canada (except for imports from Cuba and Hawaii) a higher duty than that applied to a similar import from any other foreign country.

The most-favored-nation rule still survives, but sadly shrunk in its application. Customs unions, genuine, partial, and spurious, are exempt from the rule, as are "free-trade-areas." Imports on government account never came within the rule, and with the growth of the range and volume of government trading this has become an important exception. There is no available and widely-accepted formula whereby import quotas, purchase-agreements, and the miscalled "gentlemen's agreements" could be brought under the rule even if there were any will to do so. Resort to "administrative protection" opens the way wide for nominal adherence to the rule and practical disregard of it. The rule is often not applied to the trade of a mother country with its former colonies, or to the trade between the former colonies, even when full independence has been gained by the latter, and this applies to the British Commonwealth. In the absence of the rule, each country decides unilaterally or in bilateral or multilateral bargaining on what conditions imports will be permitted entry. There is thus now a fairly wide field open for discrimination between countries, but also a wide field for preferential treatment of particular countries, on grounds of special interests, of friendship, of consideration for special needs or historical affinities or proximity, or on the basis of a negotiated mutual exchange of favors. The United States can, therefore, if it wishes, give Canada a substantial degree of preferred treatment and Canada can, if it wishes, deal likewise with the United States. Except for existing but terminable treaty obligations to third countries and to each other, each country is free from legal obligations and can find ample precedents for treating the other, unilaterally or by mutual agreement, as generously or as harshly as it pleases.

If any country, therefore, feels itself aggrieved by another country's treatment of its exports, there is today no impartial arbitrator to appeal to, and even if there were he would have no widely-accepted code of principles or rules to apply. Indeed often the smaller countries in practice have and exploit the greatest measure of freedom from external restraints on their trade-policy autonomy. If a country is small enough to be important to no other country, no other country is likely to retaliate no matter what it does. On the other hand a major trader in world markets, or with its neighbors, will expect any important restrictive action on its part to be imitated, or to be adjusted to, by countries feeling injured by its action, or even to be countered by punitive retaliation. The United States is in the second category. Canada is somewhere between the two categories.

Possibilities for negotiation

If this is a reasonably correct account of the present trade-barriers, and if Canada feels aggrieved by American treatment of her exports, what can she do about it? She can negotiate. If there is on the American side no positive malice against Canada and at least a platonic willingness to be nice to her, the United States would at any time participate willingly in such negotiations on a bilateral basis, within the limits of existing international trade obligations. In the course of such negotiations, the United States would no doubt be able to discover some grievances of her own, and would insist that a one-sided reciprocity would not be acceptable to her. If Canada were willing to negotiate on this basis, I do not see obvious advance ground for pessimism as to the results.

I do not think, however, that the proper way to lay the ground for such negotiations is to engage in advance in mutual recriminations, unilateral or reciprocal, official or unofficial. The procedure most likely to have a mutually acceptable outcome would leave most of the negotiations to the professional staffs, and as far as possible defer public declamation until the results of the negotiations were ready to be submitted for public ratification in accordance with the constitutional procedures of the two countries. The Canadian grievances, of course, could in the course of the negotiations have been presented in sober and documented fashion, or, if they were not substantial enough to be so presented, they could have been temporarily kept in storage. If the negotiation failed to remove the grievances or to expose them as ill-founded, a time more appropriate for public recriminations would have arrived. Even then they might serve no useful purpose, but they would do less harm.

But given the apparent range of present-day Canadian objectives, and abstracting from their possible validity and practicality on strictly economic grounds, what negotiations would be appropriate to the promotion of these objectives? Lowering American barriers on imports from Canada would make less "unfavorable" the Canadian balance of trade with the United States, but it would also increase the dependence of the Canadian economy and Canadian prosperity on the American market. A mutual lowering of trade barriers between the two countries would still further entangle the two economies and diminish the elements of triangularity remaining in Canada's trade relations with the outside world. It would also inevitably revive memories of the political undertones historically associated with the "reciprocity" issue in Canada. To lessen rather than to accentuate the "Canadian-American problem," Canada's negotiations on its trade relations with the United States should therefore be directed toward bettering its "terms-of-trade" with the United States and lessening its imports from the United States, but not expanding exports to the United States.

Not only would such negotiations be largely conducted with countries other than the United States, but even the negotiations with the United States would be in large part directed toward obtaining American support for Canada in its negotiations with third countries, or with trade blocs of which the United States was not a member.

It is, for example, conceivable that Canada could attain satisfaction of a wider range of her objectives, economic, noneconomic, and uneconomic, by winning admission on favorable terms to the European Common Market or to the European Free Trade Association than by obtaining more favorable tariff treatment by the United States, whether within or outside the limits of strict most-favored-nation principles.

On no doubt a more realistic level, Canada could perhaps persuade the United States, in her negotiations within and outside G.A.T.T., with the European Common Market, the European Free Trade Association, and other existing and incipient trade blocs, to carry a brief for Canada's trade interests as well as her own.

If these trade blocs have high external tariff barriers, and if their number increases, countries which are not by themselves economic giants and which are outside any bloc are in some danger of becoming economic orphans or of being forced to seek adoption on almost any terms by some bloc or other. The United States can unquestionably exercise some influence on the height of their external tariff walls. It has already somewhat committed itself to use that influence, as a "good neighbor," on behalf of the special interests of Latin America. It might be persuaded to do so on behalf of Canada also.

Invasion by investment?

Another economic area which has been made the target for Canadian high-level expostulation against American behavior, and even for hostile, or defensive, Canadian legislation, is American direct investment of capital in Canada. In this area the charges have been most clear and explicit, but the objectives sought have not, and impressive supporting evidence has not yet been collected—or revealed to the public. To explore the economic aspects of the issue an economist would, therefore, need to start nearly from scratch. The anti-American charges in this area are only incidentally directed against official American policy and action, and these get involved primarily through the way in which the American tax system and the American tariff are supposed to encourage American direct investment in Canada.

The establishment in Canada by American business of branch-plants and subsidiary companies, and the mode of operation assigned to these branches and subsidiaries by the head-offices, are the main subjects of complaint. As examples of the complaints, it is charged that branch plants operate under instructions from their head-officers or under the direction of their own executive officers (who are mostly American) to serve American or head-office economic policy even when this is counter to Canadian national policy and economic interest. The implication here is that under like circumstances independent Canadian companies would more fully pattern their operations to conform to Canadian official policy and economic interest. It seems to me somewhat improbable that the management of large domestic corporations, whether American or Canadian, are typically besieging offices of state, or using large staffs of economists, to discover what they can do for their country regardless of their profits. It is also unlikely that governments, not waiting to be asked, make it a practice to tell individual corporate managements what precisely they should do for their country. The charge that Canadian officers of an American subsidiary would be less loyal than American officers to the head-office needs convincing support by evidence and should not have been made without such evidence.

That upon occasion an American corporation when business is slack will in the interest of maximizing profits concentrate operations in its American plants is quite easy to believe, provided it is conceded that this corporation, as other corporations, may upon other occasions find it to its profit to do exactly the reverse, depending on levels of cost and levels of demand in the two markets, on the substitutibility for each other of the products of American and Canadian plants, and on a host of other factors. Once more, what is needed is evidence.

Canada should carefully consider the alternatives open to her in this field. In many cases, I am sure (and even have some supporting evidence at my command), the choice is between an American branch plant and no plant at all.

Whatever the facts may be, however, and whatever the Canadian objectives, there is no need for recriminations. No one disputes Canada's right to decide what foreign capital may enter its domain and on what terms it will be permitted to enter—although when old investment, which was permitted entry without conditions and on the presumption that it was welcome, is involved there are at least moral obligations on Canada's part to permit it to remain. I know of no instance when the United States government has pressed other countries to admit American capital, unless there was a question of competition with the capital of some third country. I believe this is true even of oil concessions. American official financial support has been given to American enterprise abroad, but never in Canada, and, I feel sure, never anywhere against the wishes of the local government. No problem for Canada in this field has yet been convincingly brought to light, except as to what capital inflow is to her advantage, and how to get it in the amounts and forms she wants. None will be pressed on her against her will. None will be withheld from her on political grounds. And if she does not like Yankee entrepreneurs on her territory, or has a limited tolerance for them, that also is completely up to her except for past commitments, explicit and implicit.

A domestic issue

This is in fact primarily a domestic Canadian issue. In the United States such matters as the rights and privileges of aliens are predominantly within state and not federal jurisdiction, and there is a substantial body of law in the constitutions and statutes of a number of states which excludes "aliens" from certain fields. Much of this is dead letter, but in the fields at least of banking and insurance the restrictions are still operative, and Canadian concerns are by chance those most affected thereby. The American restrictions on "alien" enterprise are chiefly a response to the desire of American entrepreneurs (as of all entrepreneurs ever and everywhere) to be as free as possible from competition. If the federal constitution permitted, no doubt some states would for this purpose lump firms or individuals belonging to other states of the Union with "aliens." It is evident that support comes to the campaign in Canada against American branch plants and subsidiaries from some groups of Canadian businessmen as a manifestation of their entrepreneurial protectionism in areas in which they would be the direct beneficiaries. This may not be to our liking, but it is basically an issue for Canada, not for us, to cope with, just as the right of American states to keep Canadian insurance companies from operating in their territory is an issue for us, and not for the Canadians, to handle.

Whether the scale and the manner of American business operations in Canada creates for Canada a genuine and substantial *economic* problem, and if so what remedial action it is expedient for Canada to take, should receive serious consideration only after extensive and objective research. Since such research has not yet taken place, it seems that the answers to these questions widely circulated in Canada are at least premature.

The American Reaction

A vast unawareness

How have the American people reacted to Canadian concern with Canada's commercial, financial, cultural, and political relations with the United States? It seems to me that they have not reacted at all, that they are scarcely aware even of the existence of a "Canadian-American Problem," and that the notion of the possible existence of a parallel (or reciprocal or obverse) "American-Canadian Problem" has not so far come within the scope of their imagination.

This, of course, is not quite literally true. One should first exclude, as a special group, those Americans who are of recent Canadian origin or have special Canadian affiliations of some other kind, who may be presumed to be on the average better-informed about and more interested in Canadian affairs than other Americans. One must also exclude that extremely tiny group of American scholars who have made Canadian affairs or Canadian history or Canadian sociology a special field of research, as well as the Americans living in Canada or managing from this side Canadian business operations who no doubt by this time know more about the "Canadian-American Problem" than they want to. One must also exclude a handful of American men of goodwill who, having somehow become aware of the existence of the "Canadian-American Problem," are devoting themselves, in cooperation with correspondingly small groups of Canadian men of goodwill, to explore the "problem" with a view to finding means of resolving it. Finally, I suppose there should be excluded the occupants of a giant "Canada desk" at the State Department in Washington who have been given the assignment of following closely all developments in Canadian-American relations and submitting position papers to the high officers of the Department as guidance for official American policy with respect to the problem. But this last is surmise without benefit of actual knowledge; in my academic and civil service experience I never met or heard of a specialist on Canadian affairs in Washington.

Nevertheless, even if there were today as many men assigned in Washington to work on the "Canadian-American Problem" as there should be, at a conservative estimate 99.4 per cent of the American people have either no (or the skimpiest possible) awareness of a Canadian-American problem, or of an American-Canadian problem. This state of affairs, of course, itself constitutes a major item in the calendar of Canadian grievances which constitutes the "Canadian-American Problem." As I see things, Canadians have here a genuine grievance, and the almost general determination of the American press, of the American educational system, and of the American people in general, to remain uninformed on Canadian matters, I regard as scandalous.

But what to do about it? It is the product not of malice or dislike, but of lack of interest. This lack of interest of Americans in things Canadian may in part be due to the failure of Canadians to demonstrate to them that there exist interesting Canadian things. This may apply even to the "Canadian-American Problem." The Canadian show does not hold a candle, in eloquence, violence, color, picturesqueness, exotic setting, and charismatic leadership, to the shows of a somewhat similar genre being staged in Cuba, Panama, Ghana, and other parts. Even the great American newspaper that makes the quantitatively too modest claim that it prints all the news that's fit to print will not persist in printing things that bore its readers. Canadian newspapers and news weeklies do not penetrate into the United States. I live in a fairly substantial town, with a great university and other cultural and educational institutions, and with a population of more-than-average literacy. With the aid of a professional librarian, I have just performed some research on the Canadiana resources of the libraries in this town. These are my findings (unaudited): no local library subscribes to any English-language Canadian daily; one local library subscribes to *La Presse* of Montreal (don't ask me why); no local library subscribes to any Canadian news weekly or weekly journal of opinion. The reporting of amazing, or enraging, instances of American ignorance of Canadian geography, politics, etc., is apparently a current feature of the Canadian press. I am sure, however, that even if the Canadian press strove not to exaggerate the extent of American ignorance about things Canadian, it would not have sufficient space and personnel to handle the relevant material readily available.

In the cultural field I have an easy answer: the achievement of superlative quality will in time win awareness, despite rain and hail and snow, despite national boundaries, and despite other more artificial barriers to communication.

I am not so ready with suggestions as to how American awareness of the economic aspects of the problem can be achieved by Canada. One way would be for the politicians to turn over to the Canadian civil service the task of providing the documentation for the problem, with adequate research facilities, and with the traditional freedom to adhere to professional standards of objectivity, coherence, and responsibility. All products of the Canadian civil service command the respect and attract the attention of American scholars. Another way would be to turn over the "problem" to Canadian undergraduates as a topic for a "rag" in British university style. I could even suggest some appropriate topics for banners: "Yankees go home!"; "Rescue Canadian Oil from the Texas Buccaneers"; "Canadian Jobs and Jobbery Belong to Canadian Tycoons." Advance notice to the American press and American television would ensure abundant publicity in the United States, and the injection of a measure of domestic ridicule into the Canadian publicity about the problem might not bring irreparable harm to Canada. It might even lead to the discovery that there are many Canadians, perhaps even a majority of Canadians, for whom the problem is largely sham.

Goodwill is not for scorning

One byproduct of the problem is that many Canadians, even some scholars, are casting ridicule on the traditional phenomenon of ceremonial speeches at Canadian-American gatherings which harp on the mutual goodwill of the two peoples, on the unguarded common boundary, on the common values and objectives and cultures of the two peoples. If the ridicule is directed at the naïveté of these clichés, it may perhaps be justified. But if it is directed at the sincerity of those who utter them, I would insist that it is unjust as far as Americans are concerned. The Americans may be abysmally ignorant about things Canadian; they are certainly ignorant about the history of Canadian-American political relations. They have unlimited capacity for naïveté about Canada, and for that matter about themselves. But perhaps because of their naïveté and their ignorance, their goodwill, even if it were only platonic, is genuine as an emotion and is not hypocritical. It has not, in fact, been wholly platonic. It has been weaker upon occasion than other drives: self-interest, arrogance, submission to the pressures of particular American vested interests who see promise of booty in Canada, the absence of any urge to become alert to Canadian needs, objectives, felt-grievances. But at times it has been an essential factor in leading the United States to act with special generosity to Canada on matters of some moment, or at least to act less harshly toward Canada than it does toward any other country. I am not going to present a catalogue of "benevolent" American actions toward Canada to match the Canadian catalogues of grievances which Canada suffers. But taking "benevolence" as it manifests itself in international relations, I could do so, and others no doubt could much extend my catalogue. Let me merely cite two examples relevant to the "Canadian-American Problem." A detailed survey of the American treatment of Canada in its enactment and administration of measures involving restrictions on imports into the United States would show numerous instances in which Canada has been given preferential treatment, sometimes in violation of strict most-favored-nation obligations to other countries, the preference sometimes being extended to Mexico in order to cover the deviation by a "proximity" alibi. In the selection of commodities to be subjected to import duties and in fixing the levels of duties, the most important lobby in Washington in support of liberal treatment of imports from Canada is often constituted by those very American companies who by establishing and operating branch plants in Canada are charged with being a menace to Canada.

This American goodwill is actually and potentially valuable for Canada. If there is a parallel to it anywhere in the world, except in the relations with each other of the Scandinavian countries, it has not come within my range of vision. To scorn it, wilfully or irresponsibly, or thoughtlessly to undermine or erode it, would on purely prudential grounds seem a grossly mistaken procedure for Canadians to follow. Perhaps in this respect, if in no other, the American public's lack of awareness of the "Canadian-American Problem" is not to be regretted overmuch.

Economic Relations: The Prospect

I have already made it sufficiently clear that in my opinion the most favorable future that could be wished for with respect to the "Canadian-American Problem" is that it should quietly evaporate. Whether to expect this outcome is pure fantasy I do not know, but I think I see some factors at work which would contribute to such an outcome. My appraisal of the spread and depth of the "problem" in Canada may be the consequence of a faulty sampling of the relevant literature, or of attributing excessive weight, as a reflection of and as an influence on Canadian opinion, to this literature. There are and there will ever be genuine problems in Canadian-American relations. These will give rise to frictions, debates, recriminations. Such is the nature of international relations, and even of interstate and interprovincial relations. In this sense, there is no prospect that the "problem" element will ever evanesce out of Canadian-American relations.

Normal difficulties and the *problem*

But the "Canadian-American Problem" is, and an "American-Canadian Problem" would be, a phenomenon of quite a different and potentially more ominous character. The occurrence of specific difficulties in Canadian-American relations, the feeling of specific grievances with respect to these occurrences, the voicing of these grievances, all this is as natural as breathing and, if not exceeding ordinary limits of intensity, nearly as harmless. I do not think, however, that the phenomenon I term *the* "Canadian-American Problem" is a normal phenomenon, whether in terms of the history of Canadian-American relations since, say, World War I, or in terms of the history of any pair of countries where neither one nor both of the countries is passionately hostile to the other or where the leaders of one of the countries, or of both, do not make use of the claim that the other country is systematically hostile to it, or systematically disregards its valid interests, as an instrument of domestic politics. In the "normal" situation, problems are dealt with individually as they arise, mainly by recourse to peaceful persuasion and conciliatory diplomacy, or are allowed to obsolesce. There is in the normal situation no attempt to assemble catalogues of grievances, and to fit each grievance that can be gathered into the catalogue, which then in turn is fashioned into an aggregate indictment of the other country. In the normal situation, no person of consequence charges, or implies, that the valid grievances are all basically and inherently in one direction. In the normal situation, routine recourse to the processes of diplomacy and moderate recourse to declamation on the political platform are the standard procedures for dealing with individual problems. In none of these respects is the "Canadian-American Problem" a normal phenomenon for Canada in its relations with any foreign country. Nor would an analogous American procedure be normal for the United States aside from its relations with Iron Curtain countries. It is not obviously fantastic therefore to expect that Canada will in time cease to masquerade as the aggrieved victim of a "Natural Enemy."

The "Canadian Economic Problem" would never have appeared without historical roots, and some of these roots have been convincingly identified. Why the phenomenon appeared at precisely the time it did is, however, a complete mystery to me, and it is difficult to identify a single possibly contributory factor external to Canada which underwent radical change at about the same time. As hypothesis, therefore, I grasp at the notion that the critical factor was some change in the domestic Canadian political pattern, or in the Canadian complex of national attitudes or sentiments toward its economic or political or cultural status in the world, with the United States as in many respects the dominant connection of Canada with the world at large. These hypothetical propositions lead me to suggest possible future economic developments which could operate to end the "Canadian-American Problem."

Costs and cures

As Canadians know, the most optimistic view conceivable of Canada's economic future can coexist with the most pessimistic view of the present status of the Canadian economy, locked as it is in the grip of the American octopus. Nevertheless, I would expect most Canadians not to despair of the effect on the Canadian economy of its interdependencies with the American one if in terms of growth and of prosperity Canada were moving ahead fairly steadily. Whatever their effects on Canada's economic prospects, I will assume that the steps Canada takes legislatively and the responses American business makes to Canadian legislation will operate successfully to reduce the inflow into Canada of American capital and to lower the proportion of American to Canadian ownership of Canadian industrial facilities, and that American business will increasingly substitute for outright proprietorship joint-ownership, royalty and licensing arrangements, and so forth, in conducting its Canadian business. This would be speeded up if Canadian investment funds, or European investment funds, became increasingly available in Canada relative to American investments because of relative changes between different countries in new savings, in interest rates, or in attractive prospects for new investment. I will assume also no protectionist trend in the United States but an intensification of the prevailing protectionist trend in Canada, with the normal expectancy that these two factors in combination will lower the volume of Canadian exports of raw materials, will lower the volume and value of Canadian imports of finished goods from the United States, and will thus bring the structure of Canadian-American commodity trade closer to the Canadian ideal.

If things should work out this way, they would reduce the economic stimulants to the "Canadian-American Problem," and probably at an economic cost to Canada not excessive for the sentimental gain. To the United States these changes would probably also involve some economic loss. But the United States can afford to bear it, and should bear it as gracefully as possible.

In my discussion of Canadian-American international economic relations, I have so far largely ignored the role of third countries. Should Canada find expanded export markets there, or superior sources of imports, or increased availability of capital and of entrepreneurial skills, these would lessen the ties of Canadian economy to the American. In the net, I would expect the growth of customs unions and other regional trading blocs abroad to which neither the United States nor Canada belonged to increase the economic entanglement between the two countries, by narrowing their range of trading partners. Relative growth in economic importance of the underdeveloped countries would work the opposite way, as would also disappearance of the Iron Curtain as a trade barrier.

No one can know today, however, very much about what the world trade pattern will look like a decade from now. For the near future, it seems clear that there is not available to Canada a trade-partner offering more favorable terms and with more promising prospects than the United States. Almost throughout the range of Canadian-American economic ties, the odds seem to me to be that any *contrived* lessening of these ties by either a managed increase in Canadian self-sufficiency or a managed diversion of Canadian imports or exports or financial transactions from the United States to third countries (whatever gains it may bring in terms of the Canadian national image), will have to be paid for in economic terms.

I believe the United States would not interfere in any way, except perhaps by attempts at peaceful persuasion, should Canada choose artificially to lessen her economic links with the United States. Canada in this respect has almost complete freedom of choice provided she carries out (as she would) outstanding commitments, and provided she can afford whatever economic burden her choices may involve. The United States, I am sure, Cold War considerations apart, has no policy with respect to an optimum degree of economic linkage with Canada, and no desire to retain her as a captive customer, greatly though she values the Canadian market for her goods and Canada as a field for American investment.

Even with respect to the Cold War, where the United States is rigid and demanding, there are signs that most of the free world is tired of its economic warfare aspects, sees glowing economic prospects from their abandonment, and is moving fairly rapidly toward such abandonment. If France, Britain, Western Germany do move far in that direction, so will the United States. Canada then will be free of pressure not to sell Ford cars to Russia, and free to try to persuade Russia to buy them, and one more Canadian grievance will have obsolesced.

Douglas V. LePan 

6

The Outlook for the Relationship

A Canadian View

It is not easy for a Canadian to take a general view of the relationship between Canada and the United States in a way that will both do justice to the interests and aspirations of his own countrymen and also seem interesting and persuasive to Americans.

One thing is clear about the relationship: it is something unique in the world. It is unique in the length of the border; in the multiplicity of webs that cross it; in the volume of trade done in both directions; in the closeness with which the two economies are meshed together; in the variety of problems that the two peoples have in common, ranging all the way from petty border matters to the largest issues of peace and war. But it seems to me that some of the characteristics that make the relationship unique also render it often either boring or vexatious in American eyes: Boring because the plethora of issues involved in the relationship include many which are not of the greatest consequence when judged in the perspective of the world-wide responsibilities of the United States; and vexatious because the special, the unique, nature of the relationship makes it difficult to assimilate it into any of the patterns

---

DOUGLAS V. LEPAN *has spent a good part of his career in diplomatic, military, and research capacities for the Canadian government. Until recently professor of English Literature at Queen's University, Kingston, he is now Principal of University College, University of Toronto. Among his publications are* The Wounded Prince and Other Poems *and* The Net and the Sword.

in which American policymakers from time to time endeavour to see and sort out their agenda.

If the relationship is to be handled fruitfully and without recalcitrance, what is needed is a view of it that will give it breadth and interest without abstracting too far from the particulars of which it is made up. It sometimes seems as if a cloud has settled almost permanently over the relationship between the two countries. But perhaps that very cloudiness, that apparently chronic low ceiling, can be made to yield valuable and by no means entirely dispiriting conclusions if we approach it at the right altitude and from the proper angle. Canadians and Americans share much the same civilization. Yet there is a persistent polarization between the two countries. May not these circumstances provide almost laboratory conditions for observation? If this polarization within a common culture is watched and heeded and attended to, I believe there is much that can be learned from its operations about what is happening in the world, and about how the charged and seemingly random particles are moving, colliding, and rearranging themselves. Seen in that way, the relationship may perhaps yield conclusions that will not merely be parochial to this continent but have much wider resonance.

How Alike the Two Countries Are

Subtly different as the two countries are, the similarities between them are yet very striking. Certainly from the air you would hardly be aware of difference. The Rocky Mountains, the prairies, the Great Lakes, all go their own way, paying little attention to the border; and a traveller arriving by plane, especially if he had permitted himself merely one more drink than usual, might readily be forgiven for mistaking an airport in one country (with its *lingua franca* of runways and control-towers and terminals full of glass and abstract art and only moderately controlled confusion) for an airport in the other. Shortly he might be roused from his misapprehension by a billboard reading "Bienvenu à la vieille province" or by a statue of Queen Victoria still reigning over beds of red geraniums. But these reminders that he has entered another jurisdiction are not always either very pervasive or very compelling.

There are some business men who can forget for hours at a time whether they are attendng a meeting in a boardroom in Cleveland or Toronto. It is not always that a farmer travelling along a prairie road is seized by a sense of chill and alienation as he moves across the border; the crops look the same, and the fences, and the elevators, and the wide sky. On the Pacific coast a forest engineer or a university official or a lumberman or a poet may sometimes feel that he has more in common with others who share the distinctive culture of that seaboard than he has with Canadians living beyond the barrier of the mountains. Even in Quebec, where the differences between Canada and the United States are obviously at their sharpest and most noticeable, a politician may find that with one part of his intelligence he is working on the draft of a speech to show how necessary it is that French Canadians become masters in their own house economically, while with another part he is brooding anxiously over what luck he is likely to have next week in New York when he canvasses the investment houses there for a sizable loan. If a Maritimer travels away from his own region, he may be more overcome by nostalgia for home—the salt air, the fish wharves, the shipping—and feel closer to it, as he walks along Atlantic Avenue in Boston than he would ever be likely to feel in upper Canada.

Even our most cherished national festivals in Canada can sometimes surprise with the degree of their American content. When east and west meet each year to settle the football championship in the Grey Cup final, the licenced saturnalia which is part of the show is enriched by train-loads of Canadian fans from all over the country and by a parade on the morning of the game with floats designed to show the contributions of the various parts of the country to the national identity. But a large proportion of the players on both teams will almost certainly be American imports, and the rules of the Canadian game have been progressively Americanized for decades.

An American hinterland?

It is these similarities which make it natural, and in some moods almost inevitable, for Americans to think of Canada as a northern extension of their own country, colder, rockier, wilder perhaps, but not significantly different in any of the things that really matter. It is a place where you go fishing in summer or hunting in fall or skiing in the winter, a hinterland rather than a country. It has marvellous salmon streams—although few Canadians ever see them because they are usually owned from source to mouth by wealthy syndicates, consisting as often as not either exclusively or predominantly of Americans. It is wonderfully and reassuringly rich in raw materials—pulpwood, nickel, copper, lead, zinc, iron, oil, natural gas; and why should anyone worry if for the time being entry into the United States is restricted by tariffs or quotas or other more informal but equally effective arrangements? When the moment comes and they are more needed across the border, the barriers will come down. You can be sure of that if only because these resources are already so largely in American hands.

In the meantime Canada continues to profit, remember, from the advantages of having so many branch plants and subsidiaries of American firms, which are operated for the most part from head office as impartially as if they were located in American territory. Canada profits as well, we are reminded, from being able to export its raw materials in unprocessed form, not perhaps so liberally as all Canadians would like to see but yet in very large tonnages to meet requirements across the border, there to be made up into manufactured goods, which often leave the factory in crates or cartons whose ultimate source has often been the Canadian forests! Economic processes and interests could hardly be harmonized more satisfactorily.

There is little wonder that Canada should figure so often in the American mind (as it sometimes does unexpectedly and marginally in the poems of Robert Frost) as a wilderness looming vaguely beyond the bounds of settlement. To cite what might seem to be a trifling example, I have noticed that for more than thirty years a reference to the Province of Quebec in the erudite and meticulous notes to *The Waste Land* by that great expatriate American, T. S. Eliot, was allowed to speak of "Quebec County" as though it were a county in Maine or Vermont. Recently the reference has been corrected. Perhaps the focus is beginning to grow rather sharper.

The blinkers of kindness

The attitude towards Canada that I have been trying to describe and have attributed to many Americans is not based, I am convinced, on any ill will. On the contrary, it often springs from a genuine, if somewhat imperceptive and engulfing, kindliness. I remember one morning when I was on the staff of the Canadian Embassy in Washington going to call on a senator in his office. It was not often that we permitted ourselves to deal directly with members of the legislative branch, thinking (rightly or wrongly) that we should always conduct our business through the State Department. But this was a highly local matter—it was a question of building a bridge across one of the rivers along the border—and I thought that for once it could do no harm to approach directly the senator who was most concerned. He could not have received me more cordially and was almost embarrassing in the warmth of regard he expressed for Canada and Canadians. But then he rather took me aback by saying, "You know, I have never been able to see why there should be a border between us at all, our two countries are so much alike." I knew at once that the remark was made in all innocence and kindness of heart. I was intended to receive it as it was meant, as a compliment. Yet it troubled me and has stayed in my mind ever since, because the senator, for all his generous good nature, seemed quite unaware that if the boundary were obliterated, the result in the case of a country of some 19 million people living alongside a much richer and more powerful country of almost 190 million people would not be some kind of union; it would be simply absorption.

How Different the Two Countries Are

And that would be a pity. Most Canadians would admit, I think, that Canada has not yet succeeded in creating a clearly recognizable national identity. The difficulties have been too many, the distances too great, the circumstances too unfavourable. But the great majority of Canadians would be unwilling, I think, to forgo the trials and opportunities of nationhood; and if put to the test would claim from the marrow of their bones that there is a certain tang that is identifiably Canadian, that they have caught it now and again, however fugitive it may be, and that the world would be the poorer without it. A face seen on the street, or in battle, passionate, repressed, scarred, it would seem, with the disappointments of the Highland clearances or with the inhibitions of an almost Jansenist Catholicism, marked with defeat but also with a beautiful courage. That is one thing that awaits its due celebration.

And the land itself, "this rough sweet land," that gives off an exhalation of rigour and challenge in spite of all the complacency of our cities, "the tartan of river and rock . . . the plaid of a land with little desire to buy or sell"—we may not have been true enough to it, we may not have constructed political and social and economic systems that are worthy of it and can do justice to its ringing imperatives. But it speaks to us of something known and dear. I suppose it is in the winter that the land comes most fully into its own; when the streets near the Citadel in Quebec are rid of tourists and revert to the seventeenth century, with only a solitary religious in a purple-edged cassock, or a red-sashed sergeant, crossing the thick black ice; when old Ontario farms are as drifted with snow as they were when they were first settled; when the transcontinental trains halt in Ottawa on the first stage of a journey of almost Siberian vastness and the windows are frosted and the vapour hangs and freezes in the air and the wheels are hammered and tested for the long run up to Lake Superior and then out across the wind-swept prairies.

Or the capital itself. A nineteenth-century pundit once described Ottawa as "a sub-Arctic lumbering town transformed by a stroke of Victoria's pen into a cockpit of malodorous politics." It may be, it may be. Certainly many of its streets are shabby and sorry enough. And the Parliament Buildings, though they crown the cliff above the river with a majesty of their own, present a mixture of Venetian and Romanesque and Victorian Gothic that would drive an art historian to despair and that only perhaps John Ruskin could have wholly approved of. But to a Canadian walking below them on a spring evening and listening to the carillon or startled to hear a whitethroat singing from the maples near the statue of Sir Wilfred Laurier or trying to stay awake through a long committee meeting in the Cabinet room on a summer evening, those towers speak irresistibly of what he is, of what has made him what he is, of the society he belongs to.

National independence

I must leave these details, though. For what I am trying to say is very simple: most Canadians love their own country and cherish its independence. They know instinctively how great are the problems that must be solved if Canadian nationhood is to be sustained and strengthened. In particular, they know instinctively that the implicit contract between English-speaking and French-speaking Canadians, on which the country has been so largely based, has now, for a number of reasons, been plunged in ferment; and most of them—yes, most of them, I think—realize what skill and strength and forbearance will be needed if the compact is to be reinterpreted successfully in the light of new conditions and made ample enough to accommodate the aspirations of all Canadians of whatever race or language. But that has not made them falter in devotion to their own country. This marriage between the races has not been one of convenience only. It has been invested for much more than a hundred years with the experience of trials and failures and successes shared in common. The problems of the moment, unless I am seriously mistaken, are much more likely to result in strengthening the feeling of Canadian independence than in weakening or subverting it.

Should that prove to be the case, relations across the border may become even more troubling and difficult than they have been in the recent past. But the problems that arise from the assertion of national independence are inescapable. They arise, as President Kennedy explained so eloquently in his speech in front of Independence Hall in Philadelphia on the Fourth of July, 1962, from movements all over the world that the United States throughout its history has welcomed and encouraged. "For 186 years," he said on that occasion, "this doctrine of national independence has shaken the globe—and it remains the most powerful force anywhere in the world today." It is as powerful, I would remind you, on the northern door-step of the United States as anywhere else. And if it would be irresponsible for Canadians to try to promote their own national interests without paying due regard to the interests of the wider international communities to which they belong, it would be equally illogical for Americans to encourage the spirit of national independence in Africa and Asia and yet at the same time be suspicious and intolerant of its expression in their own back yard.

Roots of difference

The differences that a Canadian senses when he thinks of his own country and of the United States have long roots. Partly they go back to the broad decision, later incorporated in statute, that the right of French Canadians to their own language and laws and religion should be protected, and to the pattern of national development that has flowed from that decision, so that Canada has become much less of a melting-pot than the United States. They go back also to the way Canadian independence was achieved—by compromise and negotiation rather than by revolution. They also owe something to the continuance of royal institutions within Canadian democracy, so that at its best our democratic ideals are personal as well as legal or philosophical, aiming not so much at the maintenance of an abstract and mathematical equality as at extending further and further the courtesy and respect to be found in a company of friends and associates. So deeply are the differences historically conditioned, that I sometimes think they can be explained, with only a little exaggeration, by the fact that the eighteenth century, which launched the United States on the world scene and provided it with its constitution and philosophy and sense of mission, virtually passed Canada by. Before 1763, French-speaking Canadians had been insulated from the century of the *philosophes* by the influence of both church and state; and later they rejected it when they rejected the French Revolution. The first English-speaking settlers rejected it as well by rejecting the American Revolution. As a result, it sometimes seems as though it had been dropped out of our history.

It has been a source of strength to the United States that it began with such a clean slate and such clear postulates. Those conditions helped to set the stage for vigorous expansion, not greatly inhibited by tradition or by preoccupying concern for racial or personal differences. But where all men are equal, all men may be equally worthless or equally open to pressure and manipulation. God knows those dangers exist in Canada! But if the dangers sometimes present themselves in subtly different forms on one side of the border from on the other, and need to be treated with subtly different remedies, the explanation principally lies in the different histories of the two countries.

So it is appropriate that historians have perhaps done more than any others to reveal Canadians to themselves and to help them know themselves for what they are. Some countries which must live in the shadow of much more powerful neighbours and are thereby almost inevitably precluded from achieving the fullest political self-expression have been able to find some measure of self-realization in the accomplishment of one or two writers or artists of genius who have epitomized much of their national life and spirit. I think of Scotland, for example, or Finland. Unfortunately, there have not yet been any Canadian composers or writers or painters whose work has been large and rich enough for Canadians to take it to themselves and use it as a rallying point for national pride. In their place, we have had a number of historians who have re-interpreted Canada's place so as to bring out admirably its special structure and flavour. Occasionally, one may feel that they have succeeded almost too well; if an explorer or a fur-trader wanders too far from the east-west routes that have been laid down for him and is deflected south of the 49th parallel, one sometimes feels that he might just as well have vanished from sight altogether! Yet Canada has been greatly indebted to its historians for informing its national life with shape and colour and for preventing it from seeming too nebulous and frustrated.

The Problems Thicken

Elsewhere in this volume the particular problems that are currently facing Canada and the United States have been examined and analyzed. They are many and various and different. And they do not grow fewer. I should like to suggest some underlying reasons why they will probably become even more numerous and more acute. One reason is the continuing internal controversy in Canada over relations between the races, over the question of whether the country properly consists of one nation or two; that controversy may have the effect of making Canadian spokesmen and negotiators more apprehensive and assertive and categorical in their dealings with other countries, and particularly with the United States, than they might otherwise be. Another reason I have just hinted at is a deep and insidious, if not always widely recognized, sense of national frustration. A country that feels its national independence circumscribed by limitations it hardly anticipated and its national aspirations baffled in ways that it hardly understands is bound to be sensitive about almost every issue affecting its interests. Canada has had full national independence for only a very few decades. There was little opportunity for it to consolidate and exploit and enjoy its independence before it was summoned by the inexorable demands of an increasingly interdependent and increasingly dangerous world. In all the circumstances it seems to me that Canada's performance has been creditable enough. But it should occasion little surprise if such a country is sometimes prickly about its interests and even sometimes peevish about its duties.

Canadians cannot help sometimes hankering for a world where things would be different. It would be pleasant if there could be more scope for an independent foreign policy, if we could settle our own defence policy more freely, if we could have a more self-sufficient economy without sacrificing the economic advantages that flow from our close association with the United States. If . . . if . . . if . . . if. If wishes were horses, Canadians would certainly ride off in all directions. To outsiders, this may all seem unreasonable and utopian and childish. So it is, if the mood comes too often or is indulged too generously. But it is also natural and human. For has not nationalism often been associated with utopian dreaming, and dreaming not always rigorously grounded in what might be feasible?

The impact of economic thought on contemporary nationalism

It will cause less surprise, I think, that Canada is at present so vulnerable to this mood and to the sense of frustration that follows in its wake if it is remembered that at a time when Canada, as a country with a relatively mature economy and with specially close ties with the United States, is being called on to temper its sovereignty to the needs of the alliance to which it belongs and to the even larger needs of a crowded and anxious and hungry planet, other countries—tens of them—are coming fresh to the heady joys of independence. Perhaps in the intoxication of the moment they may be deluded about what lies in store for them. But in the first flush of enthusiasm they draw encouragement and support from what they find in the work of contemporary economists. For thirty years economists in the western world have been explaining how national governments with responsibility for budgetary receipts and expenditures and with control over credit and currency can use those powers to maintain employment and create conditions of economic stability. That body of doctrine has provided nationalism with a new justification and a new incentive. Once attain independence, it promises, and the way will be open to controlling the economy so that every citizen may benefit. In this way, nationalism has been given a new and fuller content. Nor has it everywhere been forgotten what Marxist theorists have had to say about the possibility of economic, as distinct from, political colonialism and about the disadvantage that such a colonial economy may involve in the form both of instability and stagnation. There has also been among economists new concentration on the problems of economic growth in order to determine how it can best be promoted and what are the conditions necessary before it can become self-sustaining.

Obviously, I am not competent to work out in detail how all these trends of economic thought are combining and converging to alter the expectations now associated with the achievement of national independence. I am convinced, though, that their effects have been wide and deep. The field of action that they have sketched for deliberate national policy is so large and exciting that they have succeeded in giving almost a new meaning to national independence. Now independence seems feeble and inadequate unless it can be given economic, as well as political, expression. That is true in varying degrees everywhere in the world today. It is certainly true in Canada; and no one can understand the current climate of Canadian opinion without taking it into account.

The effects of economic penetration

It is in the light of these developments throughout the world that the continuing unease in Canada about the degree to which its industries are owned and controlled across the border should be regarded. Canadian concern on this score can fairly easily be made to seem misplaced or even ridiculous. Are Canadians unaware of how much of their prosperity has been due to the inflow of American capital? Are they unaware of how they might be injured if it were to dry up? Are they unaware of the risks involved in trying to become less dependent on flows of capital from across the border? No, they are not unaware, they are not unaware of any of these things, I think. But they continue to be worried about the scale of American ownership and control of many of their industries, including many of those that are most profitable and promising and dynamic. Insofar as they are intelligent, they would admit that this is a problem far easier to identify and analyze than to find remedies for; remedial action, unless carefully considered and designed, could easily do more harm than good. The matter is not closed with that admission, though. The nagging suspicion remains that Canada's independence is being sapped and undermined as the ownership and control of many of its most important industries falls increasingly into American hands. This suspicion can be supported, it can be controverted, it can be argued over. But what is more important, in my opinion, than any of the arguments is the fact that the deep and baffling unease in Canada over this issue is fed by the expectation, so widely shared throughout the world nowadays, that national independence, if it is to be real and satisfying, should be able to find expression in economic as well as in other terms. And that expectation, together with the developments in the Canadian economy that seem to run counter to it, provides another reason why relations between the two countries are likely to become, if anything, even more sensitive and troublesome than they have been in the recent past.

What the Relationship Requires of the Two Countries

Well, what can be done about it? What can be done to make the relationship as fruitful and creative as possible and to prevent it from becoming mired and embittered in seemingly endless squabbles and recriminations? It seems to me there was good sense in the two general suggestions with which the members of the Royal Commission on Canada's Economic Prospects concluded their chapter on "Canada and the United States."

> Such economic problems, as may arise from time to time between the two countries would be eased, in our opinion, if more Americans could remember to think of Canada, not as a hinterland but as a country. Canadians for their part, while taking such action as may be necessary to provide the economic basis for the nation they are building in the northern half of the continent, would do well to recognize how much

> they have profited from having as neighbours a people so productive, so ingenious, and so capable of magnanimity.

Both those suggestions were intended primarily to help in the solution of economic problems between the two countries. But I think that if they are pondered and perhaps amplified a little and their implications allowed to emerge, they will be found to apply more widely.

What is required of Canada

Sometimes it would seem that Canadians, for all their close familiarity with American life, persist in seeing it in terms of stereotypes—and stereotypes that are often out of date at that. They are keen to seize on indications of how acquisitive and materialistic American society is. They are not so quick to appreciate the scale of economic assistance that the United States has been giving, year after year, to so much of the world. They know about crime and violence and juvenile delinquency in American cities. They are less influenced by the youthful idealism that is being channeled into service overseas under the auspices of the Peace Corps. They follow with relish the more bizarre vagaries of American education. They do not always care to acknowledge that the best American universities are among the best in the world. They like to criticize American foreign policy when it is rash or ill-informed or a failure. They are slower to applaud when it is restrained and steady and successful. In the welter of news that pours across the border, they have difficulty—sometimes understandably, sometimes not—in distinguishing the good from the bad, the solid from the ephemeral, in recognizing that there are celebrated American architects and writers and theologians as well as spacemen and multimillionaires and film stars. How vast and varied and turbid American society is, how full it is of extremes and innovations of all kinds, that is something that Canadians are aware of in theory; but they have difficulty, some of them, in grasping the corollary that there is much there that is well worth study and imitation. It would be healthier, I think, for the relationship between the two countries, if Canadians, without compromising in any respect their right to go their own way, were to recognize more fully than they ordinarily do that within the variety of American life is to be found much of the spectrum of possibilities that the future is likely to hold out for all those who share in the civilization to which both countries belong, and more particularly, for all those who live on this continent.

To recognize that would be a mark of national self-confidence and maturity. It would rid us of some illusions and would strengthen us to work out our own destiny with greater vigour. By accepting that home truth more unreservedly we would find more freedom to be ourselves. At the same time, there would be less risk of the relationship between Canada and the United States being saddled too heavily with the frustrations that Canadians feel, both because of their own internal difficulties and because of external limitations set by circumstances on their sovereignty. To accept the circumstances in which you are placed can be a step towards accepting yourself; and accepting yourself a step towards discovering yourself; and discovering yourself a step towards creating yourself. If we in Canada could accept more confidently the special circumstances of our relationship with the United States and, in particular, could acknowledge more fully the range and vitality of American life, I am convinced that we would be more likely, not less, to give creative, positive content to our own independence. Achieving that degree of strength and self-confidence would also be likely to make us sympathize more with the world-wide responsibilities of the United States and become more forthright friends and allies.

What is required of the United States

What is required of the United States, on the other hand, if the differences between the two countries are to be handled as constructively as possible? Something, I think, at least as large and fundamental. It must come to think of Canada not essentially as a playground, not as a source of raw materials, not as a useful, if backward, annex to the domestic market, not as a *glacis* between itself and the Soviet Union, not as the great out-of-doors where some millions of squatters have unaccountably settled, not as a museum of old-fashioned qualities miraculously frozen in ice, not as any of these things, but as a country with its own problems, possibilities, desires, faults, virtues, contradictions. That will not be easy, partly because Canada is so near, partly because it is so familiar, partly because it is so like the United States, because its face does not return the shock of novelty, of otherness, so intransigently as do scores of foreign countries. Paradoxically, it may be easier for Americans to deal shrewdly and sympathetically with the problems of nationalism where they present themselves in a more exotic guise. But Canadian independence is no less intractable a fact for being a North American fact. There have always been Americans, both within and without the United States government, who have realized the importance of bearing that fact in mind when dealing with problems between the two countries. I would guess, though, that their efforts have often been hampered by those who have been beguiled from time to time by more distant and grandiose vistas and also by sheer good-natured ignorance and unconcern on the part of the public generally.

If all the United States' dealings with Canada could be coloured with some continuing concern for Canadian independence, then arguments that now often seem at cross purposes would begin to fall into place and difficulties could be more readily resolved. I hesitate to take specific examples. But in that event, it seems to me that efforts by the Canadian government to come to the rescue of the seriously dwindling number of national magazines in Canada would merit more sympathetic consideration in Washington than they have received in the past, and it would no longer seem adequate to castigate them by references to the sanctity of the principles of free trade and freedom of the press. At no point am I suggesting that particular American interests should be disregarded. What I am suggesting, though, is that concern for the independence, for the independent strength, of all its friends and allies, including Canada, should be regarded as forming part of the national interest of the United States and that it should not be overlooked in the course of particular negotiations or of general planning.

To adopt that attitude would mean that a little more room might be left for Canadian interests and aspirations by the grand designs of American foreign policy than has always been the case in the past. I suppose it is inevitable that policy planners, particularly in Washington where the problems funnel in so remorselessly, should become addicted to such grand designs; otherwise they might feel that they had little purchase on the flow of events at all. But grand designs are often obliged to leave out of account facts of almost as great importance as those they include; and they are always at the mercy of events. It may even be that the peoples of the world have had almost enough of grandeur and will begin to be content with solutions that are more provisional and tentative and piecemeal.

A Laboratory of World Problems

In that case, particularly, there may be useful lessons and reminders for American policy to be found not very far from home. For it seems to me that the relationship between Canada and the

United States is a kind of cloud chamber in which can be seen with particular clarity many of the things happening in the world today. The two countries share the same continent, the same civilization, and much the same kind of society; yet there is a persistent polarization between them; and those conditions provide almost laboratory conditions for observation. Peering into this cloudy field and watching the behaviour of the erratic particles, the observer can trace here in microcosm what is happening in many other parts of the world as well. And what will he find? A crisis of the nation-state, I think. And a crisis of change. And a crisis of power.

Crisis of the nation-state

Of recent years, there has been a great increase, as everyone knows, in the number of independent nations in the world; and the effects of this development can be seen rippling across opinion in Canada, and particularly in the Province of Quebec. Yet, at the same time, the pace of change in science and technology, not only for industrial uses but for defence as well, and the larger and more complex scale of production that it has dictated, have seemed to make it desirable, if not imperative, that groupings of people should be larger, not smaller, that the number of units should be diminishing, not increasing. And these conflicting developments in turn have been criss-crossed by the influence of economic ideas that have suggested how many opportunities for bettering their lot may be open to peoples who, in whatever ways and at whatever removes, have control over their own economic destinies. At one and the same time, national independence is coming to seem more valuable because it is acquiring richer economic content, and yet less possible because few nations are large enough or productive enough to support what it takes nowadays to be genuinely independent.

In some parts of the world a way out of this dilemma is being sought through regional arrangements; but progress in that direction is retarded by the persistence of national feelings and national wills. Meanwhile, the spawning of new independent states continues. Partly, their numbers are to be explained by the accidents involved in empires dissolving. But that is not the whole story, I think. The very circumstances that have made national independence hardly viable for most peoples have also operated to make them want it more—as a kind of protection, whether illusory or not, against forces that would otherwise seem too much for them. In a world of rapid change and alienation, and nightmare not far beyond the horizon, nationalism can be a comforting thing. It mobilizes everything that is closest and most familiar to the individual and makes the environment seem less incomprehensible and hostile. If you go to sleep with that pulled over your head, you may hope to sleep sounder and wake up safely in the morning. And that may perhaps help to explain why smaller and smaller groups of people are claiming independence for themselves.

So it is hardly an exaggeration, I think, to say that in large parts of the world today the nation-state is in crisis. There are many more nations than there used to be. But, on the average, they are much less viable. More is expected of national sovereignty. But its full exercise is more often frustrated. In consequence, political leaders and the peoples they represent find themselves drawn this way and that. These tensions are apparent not only within Canada but also in its relations with the United States. Indeed, they are one of the clearest sets of phenomena disclosed by observing the unique relationship between the two countries.

Crisis of change

The polarization between the two countries also operates to make visible the crisis of change. Of all the countries in the world, it is in the United States that the process of change is most rapid and apparent. The ways Canadians react to that gale across the border can be disconcertingly ambivalent. At times, we would like it believed that we can build earth-satellites, although only small ones or that some of our cities are growing as fast as any on the continent, except Los Angeles. At other times, we try to protect our separate individuality by stressing what is most special, even most old-fashioned, in our traditions. That oscillation of response is unsettling for our national life and has made it harder to create a recognizable national identity. But it is not only we in Canada who have exhibited such uncertainty of response. In some measure it applies to every other country in the world. It applies even within the United States. For, occasionally, Americans will confide that they would half like to live in Canada, where change seems less constant and values more settled. They might find themselves disappointed, I am afraid; but the wish is often sincere.

The truth is, I think, that in many areas the pace of change is now so extreme as to impose severe strains on everything human. It is possible to distinguish some of the driving-wheels that continue to impart impetus to change; but sometimes it seems to have moved quite outside human control; and its rhythms seem to have nothing to do with the rhythms of the pulse or the breath or even of the thinking or dreaming brain, to have nothing to do with anything that is human at all. Perhaps it is not surprising, then, that personal or national reactions to the velocity of change should not always be entirely measured or rational.

Crisis of power

Finally, there is the crisis of power. It has always been the fate of large and powerful states to be loved less than they would like to be and to be suspected more than they think they deserve. That was true of Britain in the nineteenth century. It is true of the United States today. I used to think that the operations of power and the operations of love were always antithetical. I don't think so any longer. I think they can sometimes be curiously interfoliated. But in practice, it is difficult for power and love to go together—for those who are powerful also to be loved. Power, no matter in however friendly and responsible hands it is held, inevitably attracts to it some measure of envy and suspicion and distrust on the part of those who don't possess it or are unable to share in its exercise. They are suspicious of it, worried about it, anxious about it. I say there is a crisis of power in the world nowadays because, as we can see by observing the relationship between Canada and the United States, these feelings of anxiety have been given a much sharper edge during the last few years than ever before. The power in question is now the power to destroy absolutely, to destroy whole nations, to destroy the species. When the nature of power has been transformed so radically, it is only natural that there should be a similar escalation in the anxieties felt about it.

Canadians count themselves fortunate to be friends and allies of the United States, but neither friendship nor alliance can rid them of anxiety over the absolute and awful power that rests with the United States by virtue of its nuclear armory. The latter now colours all relations across the border. I mention it, not because it is special to the relationship between Canada and the United States, but because it can be seen with particular clarity there, where otherwise everything might often seem so work-a-day and normal. It also colours, I suspect, the relationships between the United States and every other country in the world. And when power has been so utterly transformed, when the consequences of using it would be so appalling, when the responsibility for deciding on its use is already so nearly intolerable, I cannot but believe that Americans themselves will be increasingly troubled by the crisis of power and will come increasingly to insist that it should somehow be transcended.

And So . . .

These are some of the things I see, or seem to see, when I look at the clouded relationship between Canada and the United States. It is unique. It is full of difficulty. It will take much patient thought and work on both sides to handle the difficulties constructively. But it may prove easier to summon the necessary intelligence and good will if it is realized that the questions at issue are by no means all parochial. In truth, the relationship contains within itself most of the problems of the whole planet, on which we are all adrift together.

Table I

THE UNITED STATES AND CANADA, BASIC INDICATORS

	United States	Canada	Ratio U.S. to Canada
Area (millions of square miles)	3.6	3.9	1 to 1.1
Population (mid-1963, millions)	189.4	18.9	10.0 to 1
Gross National Product (1963, $U.S. billions)	585.1	38.1	15.3 to 1
GNP per capita (1963, $U.S.)	3,090	2,014	1.5 to 1
National budget (1964 estimate, $U.S. billions)	98.4	6.4	15.4 to 1
National Defense expenditures (1964 estimate, $U.S. billions)	55.3	1.53	36.0 to 1
Military manpower (thousands)	2,681	183	14.7 to 1
Total trade (1963, $U.S. billions)	38.2	12.4	3.1 to 1
Total trade per capita ($U.S.)	201.5	652.7	1 to 3.2
Canada-U.S. trade per capita ($U.S.)	42.0	401.1	1 to 9.6

Table II

MAJOR TRADE FLOWS, 1963
(Millions of $U.S.)

	UNITED STATES				CANADA			
	Exports		Imports		Exports		Imports	
	$	% *Total*	$	% *Total*	$	% *Total*	$	% *Total*
All countries	21,014	100.0	17,142	100.0	6,289	100.0	6,067	100.0
Canada	4,119	19.6	3,829	22.3	—	—	—	—
United States	—	—	—	—	3,484	55.4	4,109	67.5
European Common Market	3,949	18.8	2,517	14.7	439	7.0	316	5.2
Japan	1,697	8.1	1,438	8.7	274	4.4	121	2.0
United Kingdom	1,161	5.5	1,079	6.2	931	14.8	487	8.0

Source: U.S. Department of Commerce and Dominion Bureau of Statistics.

Table III

COMPOSITION OF CANADIAN-AMERICAN TRADE, 1963
(Millions of $U.S.)

	U.S. Exports to Canada	*U.S. Imports from Canada*
Total	$4,119	$3,829
Food and live animals	440	259
Beverages and tobacco	9	92
Crude materials, inedible[1]	367	1,070
Mineral fuels and related materials	178	343
Animal and vegetable oils and fats	15	1
Chemicals	301	236
Machinery	1,173	258
Transport equipment	551	101
Other manufactured goods[2]	933	1,259

[1] Includes lumber, wood pulp, and iron ore.

[2] Includes iron and steel mills products, pig iron, textiles, paper, nickel, and aluminum.

Source: U.S. Department of Commerce. Breakdown is by S.I.T.C. "Sections."

Table IV

MAJOR ITEMS OF CANADIAN-AMERICAN TRADE, 1963
(Millions of $U.S.)

U.S. Exports to Canada	
Grains and preparations	169
Fruits, nuts, and vegetables	172
Coal, coke, and briquettes	136
Agricultural machinery and tractors	252
Auto parts for assembly	354
Iron and steel mill products	113
Pig iron and other materials	166
Textile yarns, fabrics, and made-up articles	112
U.S. Imports from Canada	
Fish and shellfish	108
Shaped wood products (lumber)	328
Pulp and waste paper	306
Iron ore	199
Crude and partly refined petroleum	234
Chemical elements and components	164
Agricultural machinery and tractors	128
Paper and manufacturers	684
Nickel	146
Aluminum	110

Source: U.S. Department of Commerce.

Table V

MAJOR INDICATORS OF U.S. INVESTMENT IN CANADA, 1954-1963
(Millions of $U.S.)

	1954	*1955*	*1956*	*1957*	*1958*	*1959*	*1960*	*1961*	*1962*	*1963*
U.S. Direct Investment										
Value Accumulated										
In all areas	17,631	19,395	22,505	25,394	27,409	29,827	32,778	34,664	37,145	n.a.
In Canada	6,043	6,761	7,795	8,769	9,470	10,310	11,198	11,614	12,131	n.a.
Annual Outflow										
To all areas	667	823	1,951	2,442	1,181	1,372	1,694	1,475	1,557	1,799
To Canada	408	353	601	678	421	417	471	272	312	297
U.S. Portfolio Investment										
Outflow for New Issues of Foreign Securities										
To all areas	309	128	453	597	955	624	573	523	1,076	1,294[1]
To Canada	167	39	375	324	367	437	227	237	457	736[2]

[1] Of which 1,024 in first 6 months.
[2] Of which 632 in first 6 months.

Source: U.S. Department of Commerce. (1963 figures subject to adjustment.)

Table VI

U.S. OWNERSHIP AND CONTROL OF CANADIAN INDUSTRY

Industry Classification	Nonresident *ownership* as a percentage of selected Canadian industries				Nonresident *control* as a percentage of selected Canadian industries			
	1958	*1959*	*1960*	*1961*	*1958*	*1959*	*1960*	*1961*
Percentage of Total Owned or Controlled by United States Residents:								
Manufacturing	40	41	41	43	44	44	44	45
Petroleum and natural gas	56	55	53	51	67	67	64	60
Mining and smelting	47	49	52	54	51	53	53	52
Railways	10	9	9	9	2	2	2	2
Other utilities	12	12	11	11	4	4	4	4
Total of above industries and merchandising	26	26	27	27	26	26	26	26

Source: Dominion Bureau of Statistics.

Index

The American Assembly

Since its establishment by Dwight D. Eisenhower at Columbia University in 1950, The American Assembly has held Assemblies of national leaders and has published books to illuminate issues of United States policy.

The Assembly is a national, nonpartisan educational institution, incorporated under the State of New York. It was the official administrator of the President's Commission on National Goals, which reported to President Eisenhower late in 1960.

The Trustees of the Assembly approve a topic for presentation in a background book, authoritatively designed and written to aid deliberations at national Assembly sessions at Arden House, the Harriman Campus of Columbia University. These books are also used to support discussion at regional Assembly sessions and to evoke consideration by the general public.

All sessions of the Assembly, whether international, national or local, issue and publicize independent reports of conclusions and recommendations on the topic at hand. Participants in these sessions constitute a wide range of experience and competence. Over sixty institutions of higher education have cosponsored one or more regional Assemblies.

American Assembly books are purchased and put to use by thousands of individuals, libraries, businesses, public agencies, nongovernmental organizations, educational institutions, discussion meetings and service groups. The subjects of Assembly studies to date are:

1951———United States—Western Europe Relationships
1952———Inflation
1953———Economic Security for Americans
1954———The United States Stake in the United Nations
———The Federal Government Service
1955———United States Agriculture
———The Forty-Eight States
1956———The Representation of the United States Abroad
———The United States and the Far East
1957———International Stability and Progress
———Atoms for Power
1958———The United States and Africa
———United States Monetary Policy
1959———Wages, Prices, Profits and Productivity
———The United States and Latin America
1960———The Federal Government and Higher Education
———The Secretary of State
———Goals for Americans
1961———Arms Control: Issues for the Public
———Outer Space: Prospects for Man and Society
1962———Automation and Technological Change
———Cultural Affairs and Foreign Relations
1963———The Population Dilemma
———The United States and the Middle East
1964———The United States and Canada
———Congress and the American Future
1965———The Courts and the Public

American Assembly Books in the Spectrum Series

ARMS CONTROL: ISSUES FOR THE PUBLIC,* edited by Louis Henkin, S-AA-4

AUTOMATION AND TECHNOLOGICAL CHANGE,* edited by John T. Dunlop, S-AA-7

CULTURAL AFFAIRS AND FOREIGN RELATIONS,* edited by Robert Blum, S-AA-8

GOALS FOR AMERICANS: THE REPORT OF THE PRESIDENT'S COMMISSION ON NATIONAL GOALS, S-AA-3

OUTER SPACE,* edited by Lincoln P. Bloomfield, S-AA-5

THE POPULATION DILEMMA,* edited by Philip M. Hauser, S-AA-10

THE SECRETARY OF STATE,* edited by Don K. Price, S-AA-2

THE UNITED STATES AND CANADA,* edited by John Sloan Dickey, S-AA-12

THE UNITED STATES AND LATIN AMERICA (Second Edition),* edited by Herbert L. Matthews, S-AA-9

THE UNITED STATES AND THE FAR EAST (Second Edition), edited by Willard L. Thorp, S-AA-6

THE UNITED STATES AND THE MIDDLE EAST,* edited by Georgiana G. Stevens, S-AA-11

* Also available in clothbound edition.

E
183.8
.C2
A65